WRITERS ON FILE

General Editor: Simon Trussler
Associate Editor: Malcolm Page

TENNESSEE WILLIAMS
on File

Compiled by Catherine M. Arnott

Methuen. London and New York

First published in 1985 in
simultaneous hardback and paperback editions
by Methuen London Ltd,
11 New Fetter Lane, London EC4P 4EE
and Methuen Inc, 733 Third Avenue,
New York, NY 10017

Typeset in IBM 9pt Press Roman
by 🅰 Tek-Art, Croydon, Surrey
Printed in Great Britain by
Hazell Watson & Viney Ltd
Member of the BPCC Group
Aylesbury, Bucks.

British Library Cataloguing in Publication Data

Arnott, Catherine M.
    Tennessee Williams on file. — (Writers on file)
    1. Williams, Tennessee — Criticism and
        interpretation
    I. Title   II. Series
    812'.54   PS3545.I5365Z/

    ISBN 0-413-58550-6
    ISBN 0-413-54780-7 Pbk

Cover image based on a photo by Popperfoto

Contents

The theatre is, by its nature, an ephemeral art: yet it is a daunting task to track down the newspaper reviews, or contemporary statements from the writer or his director, which are often all that remain to help us recreate some sense of what a particular production was like. This series is therefore intended to make readily available a selection of the comments that the critics made about the plays of leading modern dramatists at the time of their production – and to trace, too, the course of each writer's own views about his work and his world.

In addition to combining a uniquely convenient source of such elusive *documentation*, the 'Writers on File' series also assembles the *information* necessary for readers to pursue further their interest in a particular writer or work. Variations in quantity between one writer's output and another, differences in temperament which make some readier than others to talk about their work, and the variety of critical response, all mean that the presentation and balance of material shifts between one volume and another: but we have tried to arrive at a format for the series which will nevertheless enable users of one volume readily to find their way around any other.

Section 1, 'A Brief Chronology', provides a quick conspective overview of each playwright's life and career. *Section 2* deals with the plays themselves, arranged chronologically in the order of their composition: information on first performances, major revivals, and publication is followed by a brief synopsis (for quick reference set in slightly larger, italic type), then by a representative selection of the critical response, and of the dramatist's own comments on the play and its theme.

Section 3 offers concise guidance to each writer's work in non-dramatic forms, while *Section 4*, 'The Writer on His Work', brings together comments from the playwright himself on more general matters of construction, opinion, and artistic development. Finally, *Section 5* provides a bibliographical guide to other primary and secondary sources of further reading, among which full details will be found of works cited elsewhere under short titles, and of collected editions of the plays – but not of individual titles, particulars of which will be found with the other factual data in Section 2.

The 'Writers on File' series hopes by striking this kind of balance between information and a wide range of opinion to offer 'companions' to the study of major playwrights in the modern repertoire — not in that dangerous pre-digested fashion which can too readily quench the desire to read the plays themselves, nor so prescriptively as to allow any single line of approach to predominate, but rather to encourage readers to form their own judgements of the plays, to set against the many views here represented.

The work of Tennessee Williams is in particular need of reassessment in the aftermath of his death, since during his lifetime the line between the critical judgement of a theatrical craftsman and the journalistic treatment of a phenomenon was more than usually hard to draw. Can so many of Williams's later plays have been *so* incompetently worse than those of the late 'forties and early 'fifties which established his reputation? How far were his own personal crises and the 'underground' knowledge of his homosexuality (which it only became possible for him openly to declare in his later years) contributory factors in the decline of his critical reputation?

The sheer quantity of Williams's dramatic writing makes even the contents list of this volume twice as long as any other in the series so far — and to some extent places limits on the treatment of individual plays. Many of his lesser-known works — even if one excludes, for a start, those which were precursors or reworkings or vague spin-offs of some other title — perhaps deserve no more than the brief factual treatment they receive: yet they bear witness to the sheer, compulsive energy of the writer; and some, perhaps, owed their critical dismissal as much to the fact that the public portrayal of private pain was going out of fashion as to any heavyhandedness in Williams's seemingly unending quest cathartically to translate experience into art.

More than usually, then, the reader may wish to consider the views here presented not only as individual critical judgements, but as part of that ebb and flow of a reputation created and then questioned by 'the media' in general. Though the sampling of opinion here is inevitably limited, it is dispassionately representative, and provides a necessary context in which to view the total achievement of an unevenly prolific writer who must nevertheless be accounted one of the two outstanding dramatists of the American post-war theatre.

Simon Trussler

1911 26 Mar., Thomas Lanier Williams born, son of Cornelius Coffin and Edwina Dakin Williams, in Columbus, Mississippi.

1918 Family moved to St. Louis, Missouri.

1927 First work published, a prizewinning essay in answer to the question 'Can a Good Wife Be a Good Sport?' for *Smart Set* magazine.

1928 Short story, 'The Vengeance of Nitocris', published in *Wierd Tales.*

1929 Entered University of Missouri at Columbia.

1931 At father's instigation, left university for the International Shoe Company.

1935 12 July, *Cairo! Shanghai! Bombay!* produced in Memphis, Tennessee.

1936 Enrolled in Washington University, St. Louis, Missouri. Two short plays, *The Magic Tower* and *Headlines,* produced.

1937 *Candles to the Sun* produced in St. Louis. Left Washington for the University of Iowa, Iowa City, Iowa. Sister, Rose Williams underwent prefrontal lobotomy. *The Fugitive Kind* produced in St. Louis.

1938 Graduated from University of Iowa. Submitted short plays comprising *American Blues* (*Moony's Kid Don't Cry, The Dark Room,* and *Case of the Crushed Petunias*) to play contest sponsored by Group Theatre, New York City.

1939 Awarded $100 for short plays. Audrey Wood became his agent. *Not about Nightingales* produced in St. Louis. Short story, 'The Field of Blue Children', published in *Story* magazine, his first work to appear under name Tennessee Williams. Awarded Rockefeller grant of $1000, and moved to New York City. From this year through 1944 lived for short periods in many different parts of the United States, including New York City, Provincetown, Massachusetts, New Orleans, Taos, New Mexico, and Georgia.

1940 14 Feb., *The Long Goodbye* staged in New York City. 30 Dec., *Battle of Angels* produced in Boston.

1941 11 Jan., *Battle of Angels* closed ignominiously in Boston.

1942 May, *This Property is Condemned* produced in New York.

1943 Six-month contract with Metro-Goldwyn-Mayer resulted in screenplay, *The Gentleman Caller,* the

precursor of *The Glass Menagerie.* 13 Oct., *You Touched Me,* written in collaboration with Donald Windham (his second and last collaboration with anyone) opened in Cleveland, Ohio.
1944   July, *The Purification* produced in Pasadena, California. 26 Dec., *The Glass Menagerie* opened in Chicago.
1945   25 Mar., *Stairs to the Roof* had its first and only production in Pasadena. 31 Mar., *The Glass Menagerie* opened in New York City to critical acclaim, and went on to win New York Drama Critics' Circle Award, Donaldson, and Sidney Howard Awards. 25 Sept., *You Touched Me* opened in New York.
1947   Met Frank Merlo, who became his lover and companion for the next fourteen years. 3 Dec., *A Streetcar Named Desire* opened in New York.
1948   *One Arm* published. 28 July, *The Glass Menagerie* opened in London.
1949   12 Oct., *A Streetcar Named Desire* produced in London.
1950   *The Roman Spring of Mrs. Stone* published. Film of *Menagerie* released. 29 Dec., *The Rose Tattoo* opened in Chicago.
1951   3 Feb., *The Rose Tattoo* opened in New York, to win Tony Award. Film of *Streetcar* released.
1952   *Streetcar* film won New York Film Critics' Circle Award. 24 Apr., *Summer and Smoke* opened in New York.
1953   *In the Winter of Cities* published. 19 Mar., *Camino Real* opened in New York.
1954   *Hard Candy* published.
1955   24 Mar., *Cat on a Hot Tin Roof* opened in New York, going on to win Pulitzer Prize, Drama Critics' Circle, and Donaldson Awards. Film of *The Rose Tattoo* released.
1956   *Baby Doll,* film composed in part of *Twenty Seven Wagons Full of Cotton* and *The Long Stay Cut Short,* released and immediately blacklisted by the Catholic leader, Cardinal Spellman.
1957   21 Mar., *Orpheus Descending* opened in New York. 8 Apr., *Camino Real* produced in London.
1958   30 Jan., *Cat* opened in London. 7 Feb., *Garden District* opened in New York, and on 16 Sept. in London. Film of *Cat* released.
1959   15 Jan., *The Rose Tattoo* produced in London. 10 Mar., *Sweet Bird of Youth* opened in New York. 14 Apr., *I Rise in Flame, Cried the Phoenix* produced in New York. 14 May, *Orpheus Descending* opened in London. Film of *Suddenly Last Summer* released.
1960   10 Nov., *Period of Adjustment* opened in New York. *Fugitive Kind* (film of *Orpheus Descending*) released.

1961   29 Dec., *Night of the Iguana* produced in New York. Films of *Summer and Smoke* and *The Roman Spring of Mrs. Stone* released.

1962   *Night of the Iguana* won New York Critics' Circle Drama Award. 13 June, *Period of Adjustment* became Williams's first British hit. 11 July, *The Milk Train Doesn't Stop Here Anymore* premiered at the Spoleto Festival, Italy. Films of *Sweet Bird* and *Period of Adjustment* released.

1963   The autobiographical *Remember Me to Tom* brought out by his mother Edwina. 16 Jan., *Milk Train* had its American premiere in New York. Death of Frank Merlo.

1964   Film of *Iguana* released.

1965   *Iguana* produced in England, and won London Critics' Award for Best Foreign Play.

1966   *The Knightly Quest* published. 22 Feb., *Slapstick Tragedy* opened in New York. Film of *This Property Is Condemned* released.

1967   *The Two-Character Play* premiered in London.

1968   27 Mar., *Kingdom of Earth* opened in New York after protracted wrangling between producer and playwright over the title (*Seven Descents of Myrtle,* the producer's choice, won out on Broadway). 23 June, erroneously reported murdered after a bizarre communication convinced his brother Dakin that Tennessee's life was in danger. Nov., *Sweet Bird* and *Milk Train* both produced in England. *BOOM!* (film version of *Milk Train*) released.

1969   Baptised into the Roman Catholic Church. 11 May, *In the Bar of a Tokyo Hotel* opened in New York. Committed for three months to the Renard Psychiatric Division of Barnes Hospital in St. Louis. *Last of the Mobile Hot Shots* (film version of *Kingdom of Earth,* retitled *Blood Kin* in Europe) released. Awarded Doctor of Humanities degree by University of Missouri, and Gold Medal for Drama by American Academy of Arts and Letters. Controversy over an advertisement for *Life* magazine which included an attack on Williams.

1971   *Confessional* produced in Bar Harbor, Maine. July, *Out Cry,* the rewritten *Two Character Play,* opened in Chicago. After the *Out Cry* opening Williams broke with his agent Audrey Wood, and went to Bill Barnes.

1972   Apr., *Small Craft Warnings* opened in New York. Williams won National Theatre Conference Annual Award, and given Doctor of Humanities degree by University of Hartford.

1973   Jan., *Small Craft Warnings* opened in London. 1 Mar., *Out Cry* opened in New York.

1974 *Eight Mortal Ladies Possessed* published. Williams given Entertainment Hall of Fame Award, and Medal of Honor for Literature from National Arts Club.

1975 *Moise and the World of Reason* and *Memoirs* published. 14 Aug., *The Two Character Play* finally opened in New York.

1976 20 Jan., *This Is (an Entertainment)* produced in San Francisco. 18 June, *The Red Devil Battery Sign* opened in Boston and closed after ten days. 23 Nov., *Eccentricities of a Nightingale*, rewritten version of *Summer and Smoke*, opened in New York. 17 Dec., *Red Devil* produced in Vienna. *Androgyne, Mon Amour* published. President of jury at Cannes Film Festival. *Letters to Donald Windham* published.

1977 *Demolition Downtown* produced in London, *Vieux Carré* in New York, and *Red Devil* in London. Tennessee Williams Fine Arts Center dedicated at the Florida Keys Community College, Key West, Florida.

1978 *Kingdom of Earth* and *Vieux Carré* produced in London. 5 June, *Crève Coeur* given its American premiere at the Spoleto Festival in North Carolina. *Tiger Tail*, stage version of film screenplay *Baby Doll*, produced in Atlanta.

1979 10 Jan., *Crève Coeur* given New York premiere. Victim of several muggings and general hostility from 'punks' in Key West, Florida.

1980 25 Jan., *Will Mr. Merriwether Return from Memphis?* presented in a limited run at the Tennessee Williams Performing Arts Center. 26 Mar., *Clothes for a Summer Hotel* opened in Chicago. Nov., *Some Problems for the Moose Lodge* (workshop version of *A House Not Meant to Stand)* presented in Chicago.

1981 24 Aug., *Something Cloudy, Something Clear* produced in New York.

1982 8 May., *A House Not Meant to Stand* produced in Chicago. June, *Now the Cats with Jewelled Claws* commissioned by the New World Festival of the Arts, rejected on the grounds that it was too short. *It Happened the Day the Sun Rose* and *The Bag People* published. Williams celebrates seventieth birthday.

1983 24 Feb., Williams found dead in his rooms at the Hotel Elysée, New York City; coroner found that he had choked to death on a plastic cap such as that found in a nasal inhaler. *Tennessee Williams: an Intimate Biography*, written by his brother Dakin and Shepherd Mead, published.

Moony's Kid Don't Cry

Play in one act.
Written: 1934.
First production: Straight Wharf Th., Nantucket,
  Massachusetts, Summer 1946 (dir. and des. Albert
  Penalosa; with Rita Gam as Jane and Penalosa as
  Moony).
Television production: Three by Tennessee, 'Kraft
  Television Theatre', NBC-TV, 16 Apr. 1958 (dir.
  Sidney Lumet).
Published: Best One-Act Plays of 1940, ed. Margaret
  Mayorga (New York: Dodd, Mead, 1941); and in
  American Blues.

*Moony, a labourer, cradles his son in his arms and paces
the kitchen linoleum dreaming of the great outdoors.*

Cairo! Shanghai! Bombay!

Play in one act.
Written: 1935, in collaboration with Dorothy Shapiro.
First production: Rose Arbor Playhouse, Memphis,
  Tennessee, 12 July 1935 (dir. Arthur B. Scharff).
Unpublished.

*A short play about two sailors on shore leave who pick
up a couple of prostitutes.*

Candles to the Sun

Play in one act.
Written: 1935.
First production: Wednesday Club Auditorium, St. Louis,
  Missouri, 18 and 20 March 1937 (dir. Willard H. Holland).
Unpublished.

*A drama of 'poverty, degeneracy, accidents on the fifth
level below ground, a strike and a hotel murder, ending*

with beans for everybody, hope, and the singing of "solidarity forever".'

St. Louis Post-Dispatch, quoted in Edwina Dakin Williams,
Remember Me to Tom (1963)

In the depression days, all young writers thought they should be preaching social significance. (In fact, it was hard to get a grant from the WPA Writer's Project if you didn't.) This was Tom being socially significant about Alabama miners, about whom he knew nothing.

Dakin Williams and Shepherd Mead,
Tennessee Williams: an Intimate Biography, p. 51

Headlines

Sketch.
Written: 1936.
First production: Wednesday Club Auditorium, St. Louis,
Missouri, 11 Nov. 1936 (dir. Willard H. Holland). *Unpublished.*

A pacifist sketch which served as curtain-raiser for Irwin Shaw's Bury the Dead.

The Magic Tower

Play in one act.
Written: 1936.
First production: Webster Groves, Missouri, Oct. 1936 (dir. David
Gibson). *Unpublished.*

It treats of the love of a very young, not too talented artist and his ex-actress wife. ... They call the garret in which they live their 'magic tower' and are happy there until the artist's belief in his star fails. Then the magic tower becomes a dark garret once more; and tragedy, like a gray woman, glides in, to remain.

St. Louis Star-Times, 19 Oct. 1936,
quoted in *Remember Me to Tom*

Fugitive Kind

Play in one act.
Written: 1936-38.
First production: Wednesday Club Auditorium, St. Louis,
    Missouri, Dec. 1937 (dir. Willard H. Holland).
First New York production: 1939. Unpublished.

*A short play set in a men's flophouse, the title of which — and
nothing else — was borrowed for the film version of* Orpheus
Descending.

Me, Vashya!

Written: 1937. Unperformed. Unpublished.

*A wartime munitions magnate disposes of his rival in a love triangle
by having him shipped to the front.*

Spring Storm

Play in two acts.
Written: 1937. Unperformed. Unpublished.

'A tragedy of sex relations ...' had another title, April is the
Cruellest Month.... *It tells of the lovemaking of two couples,
and makes it seem rather unpleasant.*
Williams and Mead, Tennessee Williams, p. 70

Not about Nightingales

Play in one act.
Written: 1938-39.
First production: St. Louis, 1939. *Unpublished.*

Not about Nightingales *dealt with a prison riot that actually occurred at that time after a group of convicts was literally burned alive while being 'disciplined' in an oven-hot room.*

Edwina Dakin Williams, *Remember Me to Tom*, p. 97

Battle of Angels

Play in two acts.
Written: 1939.
First production: Wilbur Theater, Boston, Massachusetts, 30 Dec. 1940 (dir. Margaret Webster; des. Cleon Throckmorton; with Wesley Addy as Val and Miriam Hopkins as Myra).
Published: Murray, Utah: *Pharos*, Spring 1945; New York: Dramatists Play Service, 1975; and in *Theatre, Vol. I.* This play was revised as *Orpheus Descending*, (see page 42), and produced under that title in 1957.

Mr. Tennessee Williams has certainly written an astonishing play, one of the strangest mixtures of poetry, realism, melodrama, comedy whimsy, and eroticism that it has ever been our privilege to see upon the boards. . . . There is something for every taste and equally something that will irritate every customer who more or less knows his mind about theatrical matter. . . . Mr. Williams's hero is Val Xavier, whose 'eyes shine like a dog's in the dark.' . . . He has ever been a lonely one of the earth and lived and known love in the bayous of Tennessee. He is also writing a great book. . . . He tells his story to the heroine, Myra, the shopkeeper's wife. . . . Myra's husband is upstairs with an incurable disease . . . it later appears that he is the personification of death, and very well he succeeds in his mission on earth. Meanwhile, Myra and Val are knowing a brief interlude of happiness; and Myra, who has always feared the idea of barrenness, is going to have a child by Val. But the gossips of the town and the bad woman, Cassandra Whiteside — you catch her place in the allegory? — have also fallen for Val's charms. . . . The husband . . . now enters the picture. . . . Myra is shot, and an angry crowd assembles to burn up the house with Val in it. . . . [Cassandra] tells Val that self-immolation is to be their glorious doom.

Alexander Williams, *The Boston Herald*, 30 Dec. 1940

At Liberty

Play in one act.
Written: before 1940.
First production: New York City, Sept. 1976.
Published: in *American Scenes,* ed. William Kozlenko (New York: John Day Co., 1941).

The ageing ingenue Gloria Bessie Greene fights her tuberculosis at the expense of her reputation and, dying, rages against the confinement represented by her mother and Blue Mountain, Mississippi.

The Long Goodbye

Play in one act.
Written: 1940.
First New York production: New School for Social Research, 14 Apr. 1940.
Revived: Two One Act Plays, Straight Wharf Theatre, Nantucket, Massachusetts, Summer 1946.
Published: in *27 Wagons Full of Cotton;* and in *Theatre, Vol. VI.*

A possible precursor of The Glass Menagerie, *the play concerns a young man lost in reverie as movers empty his apartment of furniture and personal history. The sister here is a tougher, harder woman, and the mother a completely tragic figure, but the point and the impetus of the play is still the narrator's inability to leave his sister behind him.*

The Purification

Play in one act.
Written: Summer 1940.
First productions: Pasadena Laboratory Theatre, Pasadena, California, July 1944; Theatre '54, Dallas, Texas, May 1954 (dir. Margo Jones; des. Sarah Cabell Massey; with James Field as the Son).
First New York production: Th. de Lys, 8 Nov. 1959 (dir. Tom Brennan; music and choreography by Sharon Young and

Michael Childs; with Ted Von Briethaysen as the Son).
Revived: Mama Gail's, New York City, Dec. 1975.
Television production: in *Three by Tennessee*, PBS-TV, 6 Feb.
   1961.
Published: in *27 Wagons Full of Cotton;* and in *Theatre, Vol VI.*

'A play in verse to be performed with a musical accompaniment on the guitar.' An operatic poem, telling the tragedy of a brother and sister, their love, and her death, set in the nineteenth-century American West.

The Dark Room

Play in one act.
Written: c.1940.
First production: London, 1966.
Published: in *American Blues.*

A teenage Italian girl is kept locked away from the world by her family and visited nightly by the boy who got her pregnant.

Stairs to the Roof

Play in three acts.
Written: 1940-42.
First production: Pasadena Playhouse, Pasadena, California,
   25 Mar. 1945 (dir. Margo Jones). *Unpublished.*

A fantasy about Williams's three years in the warehouse of the International Shoe Company, and his longing to get out.

A symbolic representation of the struggle of the 'little man' . . . a cast of forty and twenty scenes, with sets designed especially for constantly changing 'mood' lighting, and periodic mood music rendered by recordings.
                              New York Times, 26 Feb. 1947

The Case of the Crushed Petunias

Play in one act.
Written: 1941.
First production: Shelterhouse Th., Cincinnati, Ohio, 31 May
    1973 (dir. Pirie MacDonald).
Published: in *American Blues.*

---

*An allegory: Dorothy Simple, a Massachusetts maiden lady, fences
off herself and her heart behind two rows of powerfully proper
flowers. A young pagan tramples her petunias underfoot to break
down the barrier; when the play ends Dorothy is heading for an
assignation with the stranger, travelling on a highway that leads
four ways at once.*

I Rise in Flame, Cried the Phoenix

Play in one act.
Written: 1941.
First New York production: Th. de Lys, 14 Apr. 1959 (dir.
    Tom Brennan; with Alfred Ryder as D.H. Lawrence, Viveca
    Lindfors as Frieda, and Nan Martin as Brett).
First London production: 1971.
Television production: in *Four From Tennessee,* 'Play of the
    Week', PBS-TV, 6 Feb. 1961.
Published: New York: New Directions, 1951; in *Dragon Country;*
    and in *Theatre, Vol. VII.*

---

*The death song of D.H. Lawrence, burning with consumption and
declaiming to the last his combative views on art and sex.*

Lawrence felt the mystery and power of sex, as the primal life
urge, and was the life-long adversary of those who wanted to keep
the subject locked away in the cellars of prudery. Much of his
work is chaotic and distorted by tangent obsessions, such as his
insistence upon the woman's subservience to the male; but all in
all his work is probably the greatest monument to the dark roots

of creation.

Williams, Author's Note, reprinted in *Theatre, Vol. VII*

Auto Da Fé

Play in one act.
Written: c.1941. *No professional production.*
Published: in *27 Wagons Full of Cotton;* and in *Theatre, Vol. VI.*

A porch scene between New Orleans fanatics: a spiritual mother and her asthmatic, ascetic son, Eloi, who raves about the corruption of the Old Quarter, his body and his spirit, and ends by burning down the house.

The Frosted Glass Coffin

Play in one act.
Written: c.1941.
First production: Waterfront Playhouse, Key West, Florida, 1 May 1970 (dir. Tennessee Williams).
First professional production: Alliance Theatre, Atlanta, Georgia, 11 Feb. 1980 (dir. Gary Tucker; des. Nick Mancuso; with Jim Loring as One, Leonard Shinew as Two).
Revived: Goodman Th., Chicago, 8 Nov. 1980 (dir. Gary Tucker; des. Joseph Nieminski; with Nathan Davis as One, Les Podewell as Two).
Published: in *Dragon Country;* and in *Theatre, Vol. VII.*

Small soliloquies delivered by old people on old people outside a cheap luncheonette in Miami, Florida.

Hello from Bertha

Play in one act.
Written: c.1941.
Television production: in *Four From Tennessee*, 'Play of the Week', PBS-TV, 6 Feb. 1961 (with Maureen Stapleton as

Bertha.)
Published: New York: New Directions, 1945; in *27 Wagons Full of Cotton;* and in *Theatre, Vol. VII.*

The play depicts one of the last days of Bertha, an East St. Louis prostitute, and her last message, left unsent, to a former customer.

This Property is Condemned

Play in one act.
Written: before 1942.
First New York production: New School for Social Research, May 1942.
Revived: Three Premieres, Cherry Lane Th., 28 Oct. 1956 (dir. Charles Olsen; with Billy James as Tom and Sandra Kolb as Willie).
First London production: Arts Th., 25 Aug. 1960.
Television production: in *Three by Tennessee,* 'Kraft Television Theatre', NBC-TV, 16 Apr. 1958 (dir. Sidney Lumet). *Film* (not acknowledged by Williams): Seven Arts/Ray Stark, 1966 (dir. Sydney Pollack; with Natalie Wood and Robert Redford).
Published: in *American Scenes,* ed. William Kozlenko (New York: John Day, 1941); in *27 Wagons Full of Cotton;* and in *Theatre, Vol. VI.*

Little more than . . . a haunted monologue in the Williams tradition. . . . It is the portrait of a Southern waif along a railroad embankment in Mississippi, a pathetic little waif who has been raised in a house that took in railroad men. The main attraction of that house, as she proudly boasts, was her sister, and she leaves no doubt as to the reason.

Lewis Funke, *New York Times,* 29 Oct. 1956

The Lady of Larkspur Lotion

Play in one act.
Written: before 1942.
First production: Monceau Th., Paris, 8 July 1949.
First New York production: Lolly's Th. Club, 6 Dec. 1963 (dir.

Dick Garfield, Cindy Kaplana).
Television production: in 'Play of the Week', PBS-TV, 6 Feb.
1961 (with Jo Van Fleet as Mrs. Harwicke-Moore).
Published: in *Best One-Act Plays of 1941,* ed. Margaret
Mayorga (New York: Dodd, Mead, 1942); in *27 Wagons Full
of Cotton;* and in *Theatre, Vol. VI.*

*Set in a decrepit French Quarter rooming house, this play deals
with two dreaming tenants. One, the Lady, clings to an entirely
imaginary past on a rubber plantation; the other, the Writer,
aspires to his personal fantasy of world-wide fame.*

You Touched Me

Play in three acts, based on the short story by D.H. Lawrence.
Written: with Donald Windham, 1942-43.
First production: Playhouse, Cleveland, Ohio, 13 Oct. 1943 (dir.
Margo Jones).
First New York production: Booth Th., 25 Sept. 1945 (dir.
Guthrie McClintic and Lee Shubert; des. Motley; with
Montgomery Clift as Hadrian, Marianne Stewart as Matilda
Rockley, and Edmund Gwenn as Cornelius Rockley).
Published: New York: Samuel French, 1947.

*Playwrights Williams ... and Windham are soapboxing for Life,
Growth, Fulfilment, and the Future. They set these abstractions
up in an English country house, and arrange a match against
Stagnation, Snobbishness, the Status Quo, Prudishness and Decay.
On Life's side, along with a young flyer, is the young heroine's
father ... a rum-soaked old sea captain full of Elizabethan
gusto. . . . On Stagnation's side is the heroine's aunt . . . a snooping
spinster full of Victorian gentility. . . . Almost everything the old
maid does smacks of melodrama, almost everything the old soak
does smacks of farce. ...* You Touched Me *is a gallimaufry of
didactic speeches and romantic flourishes, with the authors so
busy extolling life that they do little to create it.*

Time, 8 Oct. 1945

Had not Mr. Williams written *The Glass Menagerie* and thus proven what he could do, it would be called promising. Facts being what they are, however, the play is disappointing ... not only as an example of Mr. Williams's recent work, but as two evening hours spent at the theatre.

Lewis Nichols, *New York Times,* 30 Sept. 1945

Maybe Lawrence would be a little confused by all that has happened to his little story but that old goat, luckily, is beyond all confusion.

Williams, to Donald Windham, 20 July 1942, in
Letters to Donald Windham

The Gentleman Caller

Screenplay.
Written: under six-month contract with Metro-Goldwyn Meyer, 1943.

Seminal version of The Glass Menagerie.

Have finished *The Caller.* No doubt it goes into my reservoir of noble efforts. It is the *last* play I will try to write for the now existing theatre.

Postscript to letter to Donald Windham, Aug. 1944,
quoted in *Letters to Donald Windham*

The Glass Menagerie

Play in one act.
Written: 1943, as a revised version of *The Gentleman Caller* (see above).
First production: Civic Th., Chicago, Illinois, 26 Dec. 1944 (dir. Eddie Dowling and Margo Jones; des. Jo Mielziner; with Laurette Taylor as Amanda and Julie Haydon as Laura).
First New York production: Playhouse Th., 31 Mar. 1945 (with the same credits).
First London production: Th. Royal, Haymarket, 28 July 1948 (dir. John Gielgud; des. Jo Mielziner; with Helen Hayes as

Amanda and Frances Heflin as Laura).

Revived: New York City Center Th., 21 Nov. 1956; National Th., Washington, D.C., Mar. 1961; Brooks Atkinson Th., New York City, 4 May 1975; Circle in the Square, New York City, 18 Dec. 1975; Shaw Th., London, 13 June 1977; O'Neill Th., New York City, 1 Dec. 1983.

Film version: Warner Brothers, 1950.

Television version: CBS-TV, 8 Dec. 1966 (dir. Michael Elliott); ABC-TV, 16 Dec. 1973 (dir. Anthony Harvey; with Katherine Hepburn as Amanda and Joanna Miles as Laura).

Published: New York: Random House, 1945; London: John Lehmann 1948; in *Four Plays;* and in *Theatre, Vol I.*

A collection of glass animalculae means a great deal too much to Laura, an introvert whose shyness is enhanced by a limp and whose youth and beauty are being wasted on daydreams. Her mother, an old Southern Belle in reduced circumstances, entertained in her youth no less than seventeen gentlemen callers at a sitting, and is understandably anxious that her daughter should have at least one. The son of the house produces him – a colleague from the warehouse. . . . The newcomer was Laura's chief childhood hero, and there is a touching scene of tenderness between them which cannot, however, lead to the desired acquisition by Mrs. Wingfield of a son-in-law, for the stranger's affections are already engaged. . . . We leave the family very much where they were to start with. . . .

Peter Fleming, *The Spectator,* 6 Aug. 1948

A strict perfectionist could easily find a good many flaws. There are some unconnected odds and ends, . . . snatches of talk about the war, bits of psychology, occasional moments of rather flowery writing. But Mr. Williams has a real ear for faintly sardonic dialogue, unexpected phrases and affection for his characters. . . . Everything fits. *The Glass Menagerie,* like spring, is a pleasure to have in the neighborhood.

New York Times, 2 Apr. 1945

Is it as good as it was? Or rather is it as good as we thought it was? . . . It is still a magnificent play . . . a play about leaving and a play about survival. . . . In this play, of heart, of spirit, there was once a new dawn for the American theatre. And, naturally, dawns always survive.

Clive Barnes, New York Times, 19 Dec. 1975

She [Amanda] was a little woman of great but confused vitality clinging frantically to another time and place.... She is not paranoic, but her life is paranoia. There is much to admire in Amanda, and as much to love and pity as there is to laugh at.

Williams, notes to the play

On the Broadway opening night of *Menagerie,* the performers took bow after bow, and finally they tried to get me up on the stage.... And I felt embarrassed; I don't think I felt any great sense of triumph. I think writing is continually a pursuit of a very evasive quarry, and you never quite catch it.... [My goal in writing] is just somehow to capture the constantly evanescent quality of existence.... When I was writing *Menagerie,* I did not know that I was capturing it, and I agree with Brooks Atkinson that the narrations are not up to the play. I didn't feel they were at the time, either.

Williams, Memoirs, p. 84

I think it is high time the ghost of Amanda was laid to rest. I am *not* Amanda. I'm sure if Tom stops to think, he realizes I am not.

Edwina Dakin Williams, Remember Me to Tom

The Long Stay Cut Short
or The Unsatisfactory Supper

Play in one act.
Written: before 1945.
First production: London, 1971.
Published: as *The Unsatisfactory Supper,* in *Best One-Act Plays of 1945;* as *The Long Stay Cut Short,* in *American Blues.*

Summer and Smoke

Play in two acts.
Written: beginning of 1945; rewritten 1951 as *Eccentricities of a*

Nightingale (see p. 35).

First production: Theatre 47, Gulf Oil Playhouse, 8 July 1947
(dir. Margo Jones; with Katherine Balfour as Alma Winemiller
and Tod Andrews as John Buchanan, Jr.); Music Box Th.,
Dallas, Texas, 6 Oct. 1948 (dir. Margo Jones; des. Jo Mielziner;
with Margaret Phillips as Alma Winemiller and Tod Andrews as
John Buchanan, Jr.).

First New York production: Circle in the Square, 24 Apr. 1952
(dir. Jose Quintero; des. Keith Cuerden; with Geraldine Page as
Alma Winemiller and Lee Richard as John Buchanan, Jr.).

First London production: Lyric Th., 22 Nov. 1951 (dir. Peter
Glenville; des. Reece Pemberton and William Chappell; with
Margaret Johnston and William Sylvester).

Revived: Roundabout Stage One, New York, 16 Sept. 1975.

Film version: Paramount, 1961 (dir. Peter Glenville).

Operatic version: St. Paul Opera, St. Paul, Minnesota (dir. Frank
Corsaro; with libretto by Lanford Wilson and music by Lee
Hoiby).

Published: New York: New Directions, 1948; London: John
Lehmann, 1952; in *Four Plays;* and in *Theatre, Vol. II.*

---

*Alma Winemiller, the daughter of a Mississippi minister and his
insane wife, is a spiritually energetic girl in love with her lifelong
neighbour, Dr. John Buchanan. The young doctor is attracted by
the girl's idealism, but he expresses his tenderness towards her by
a harsh insistence on its nonspiritual aspects. Shocked, the girl
tries to pit her idealism against the boy's wasteful sinfulness. . . .
Redeemed from his carnal course, John does not turn to his
saviour Alma, but instead marries a buxom little female of coarser
background. Alma, in turn, converted to a doctrine of the senses
(reversing the pattern of ladies from Thais to Sadie Thompson),
now seems prepared to indulge in casual affairs. . . .*

In *Summer and Smoke,* so much time is given to a conscious
exposition of theme that Williams loses the specific sense of his
people and to a dangerous extent our concern as spectators . . .
the play alternates between psychoanalytic 'hints' (never artistic-
ally convincing) and what becomes . . . an almost trite and badly-
constructed plot line. Fragments of true feeling have been attenu-
ated and vitiated by the author's failure to find a proper form for

them, to think his problem through.

Harold Clurman, *New Republic,* 25 Oct. 1948

This is a tone poem in the genre of *The Glass Menagerie* and *A Streetcar Named Desire* ... the same mystic frustration and the same languid doom. So far Mr. Williams has been writing variations on the same theme. ... Mr. Williams is full of scorn for the rootless people he pities. He will not raise a finger to help them.

Brooks Atkinson, *New York Times,* 7 Oct. 1948

A Streetcar Named Desire

Play in three acts.
Written: beginning in 1945.
First New York production: Barrymore Th., 3 Dec. 1947 (dir. Elia Kazan; des. Jo Mielziner and Lucinda Ballard; with Jessica Tandy as Blanche du Bois, Kim Hunter as Stella Kowalski, and Marlon Brando as Stanley Kowalski).
First London production: Aldwych Th., 12 Oct. 1949 (dir. Laurence Olivier; des. Jo Mielziner and Beatrice Dawson; with Vivien Leigh as Blanche, Renee Ackerson as Stella, and Bonar Colleano as Stanley).
Revived: City Center Th., New York City, 23 May 1950; Originals Only Playhouse, 3 Mar. 1955; Cocoanut Grove Playhouse, Miami, Florida, 16 Jan. 1956; City Center Th., New York City, 15 Feb. 1956; McCarter Th., Princeton, New Jersey, 13 Nov. 1964; Ahmanson Th., Los Angeles, 28 Mar. 1973; Vivian Beaumont Theatre, New York City, 26 Apr. 1973; Piccadilly Th., London, 14 Mar. 1974; McCarter Theatre, Princeton, New Jersey, 7 October 1976.
Television version: ABC Theatre, 4 Mar. 1984 (dir. John Erman; with Ann-Margaret as Blanche, Beverly D'Angelo as Stella, and Treat Williams as Stanley).
Ballet: Her Majesty's Th., Montreal, 9 Oct. 1952 (choreographed by Valerie Bettis; with music by Alex North); Century Th., 8 Dec. 1952 (conducted by Otto Frolich); Dance Th. of Harlem at City Centre Th., New York, 14 Jan. 1982 (choreographed by Valerie Bettis).
Published: New York: New Directions, 1947; London: John Lehmann, 1949; in *Four Plays;* and in *Theatre, Vol. I.*

Stanley Kowalski, a tough common sexy Polish-American, and his wife Stella, who comes from a decayed upper-class family, live in Elysian Fields, a shabby riverside district of New Orleans. Stella's sister, Blanche du Bois, a brittle, prinked-up, faded beauty, disdainfully takes refuge here, and nourishes her dreams of happiness and respectability on the bottle, hot baths, romantic or neurotic passes at Stanley and his neighbours, and, above all, by dramatizing in conversation her past life. . . .

In [*The Glass Menagerie*] the heroine lived in a world of illusion, and she became as remote from life and as fragile as her own glass animals; the hero was a manufacturer of dreams, who picked the lock of his trap with symbols, and came to his truth by the path of illusion. Blanche du Bois is an ill-fated member of the same family. . . . It is this terrible loneliness, this solitary agony, that we feel unbearable. By comparison with this horror, the violent incidents of the plot — the drunken brawling, the lovemaking, the bad language — are seen (or should be seen) as subsidiary evils committed by people who are themselves not evil, who, indeed, in some important qualities, are positively good.

After this remarkable if imperfectly achieved piece Mr. Williams will either develop more positive values, or decline into the most successful playwright of our day.

R.D. Smith, *New Statesman*, 22 Oct. 1949

Like *The Glass Menagerie*, the new play is a quietly woven study of intangibles. But to this observer it shows deeper insight and represents a great step forward towards clarity. And it reveals Mr. Williams as a genuinely poetic playwright, whose knowledge of people is honest and thorough and whose sympathy is profoundly human. . . . By the usual Broadway standards, *A Streetcar Named Desire* is too long; not all those words are essential. But Mr. Williams is entitled to his own independence.

Brooks Atkinson, *New York Times*, 4 Dec. 1947

At the corner of St. Ann and Royal [Williams] is almost hit by a bus named Desire. 'Sad, sad', he shakes his head, 'it replaced the old streetcar years ago. You know I took quite a bit of poetic licence in that play. If you follow the instructions in the play and take that Streetcar, it never went to a place called Elysian Fields, and even if it did, you wouldn't be in the Quarter anymore. I used it because I liked the name Elysian Fields.'

Rex Reed, interviewing Williams in *Esquire*, Sept. 1971

Twenty-Seven Wagons Full of Cotton

Play in one act.
Written: before 1946, adapted from a short story of 1936.
First production: Tulane University, New Orleans, Louisiana, 18 Jan. 1955 (dir. Edward Ludlam; des. George Hendrickson and Homer Pouport; with Paul Ballantyne as Jake Meighan, Maureen Stapleton as Flora Meighan, and Felice Orlandi as Silva Vacarro).
First New York production: Playhouse Th., 19 Apr. 1955 (dir. Vincent J. Donahue; des. Eldon Elder and Pat Campbell; with Myron McCormick as Jake Meighan, Maureen Stapleton as Flora Meighan, and Felice Orlandi as Silva Vacarro).
Revived: Phoenix Th., New York, 26 Jan. 1976.
Film version: as *Baby Doll*, Warner Brothers, 1956 (dir. by Elia Kazan).
Published: in *Best One-Act Plays of 1944*, ed. Margaret Mayorga; New York: Dodd, Mead, 1945); in *27 Wagons Full of Cotton*; and in *Theatre, Vol. VI*.
Film Script: London: Secker and Warburg, 1957.

Williams combined this play with *The Long Stay Cut Short* (see p.23) to create the screenplay, *Baby Doll*, in 1956, from which he then developed the stage play *Tiger Tail* (see p. 64) in 1978.

There is something of a de Maupassant in him . . . the short story is a form that suits Mr. Williams unusually well. . . . Jake, the ageing owner of a cotton gin in the South . . . tries a little arson, burning down the competitor's mill, and, as a result, finds himself with 27 wagons full of cotton to gin for the syndicate. The superintendent of the syndicate, Silva, is suspicious of Jake, but finds a complaisant bed partner in Jake's wife, Flora . . . Both Jake and Silva, to say nothing of Flora, tacitly agree to adopt a 'good neighbour' policy – it is cynical, raunchy, and yet with a touch of the poet.

Clive Barnes, *New York Times*, 27 Jan. 1976

What's our finest living dramatist doing mucking about with arson, political violence, gunplay in shady roadhouses? We don't need that sort of thing in an artist, do we? In point of fact, we do. . . . Mr. Williams has got the truth of devious, vengeful, vulnerable, and calculating human beings out of a situation, an essentially melodramatic situation, faced straightforwardly. . . .

Walter Kerr, *New York Times*, 8 Feb. 1976

The Last of My Solid Gold Watches

Play in one act.
Written: before 1946.
First production: Laboratory Theatre, Los Angeles, California, 1947.
First major production: Dallas Theatre '48, Dallas, Texas, 1948 (dir. Margo Jones; with Vaughan Gloser as Charlie Colton and Tod Andrews as Bob Harper).
Television version: Three by Tennessee, 'Kraft TV Theatre', NBC-TV, 16 Apr. 1958 (dir. Sidney Lumet; with Thomas Chambers as Charlie Colton and Gene Saks as Bob Harper).
Published: in *Best One-Act Plays of 1942,* ed. Margaret Mayorga (New York: Dodd, Mead, 1943); in *27 Wagons Full of Cotton;* and in *Theatre, Vol. VI.*

Poignant picture of a fading travelling salesman in a lonely hotel room.

Portrait of a Madonna

Play in one act.
Written: before 1946.
First production: Actors' Laboratory Th., Los Angeles (Las Palmas), California, 1946-47 (dir. Hume Cronyn; with Jessica Tandy as Lucretia Collins).
Revived: Arena Stage, Washington, D.C., 19 March 1957 (dir. John O'Shaughnessy; des. Robert Conley, Leo Gallenstein, and Jane Stanhope; with Dorothea Hammond as Lucretia Collins).
First New York production: Playhouse Th., 15 Apr. 1959 (dir. Hume Cronyn; des. David Hayes and Anna Hull Johnstone; with Jessica Tandy as Lucretia Collins).
Published: in *27 Wagons Full of Cotton;* and in *Theatre, Vol. VI.*

Interesting principally in an academic sense, unless there are some who have never met Blanche Du Bois.... Lucretia Collins in Portrait of a Madonna *is Blanche with a few variations — a genteel product of the Old South who persists in maintaining her pretensions in the face of overwhelming squalor, and whose mind eventually gives way to the point that she must be committed to a sanitarium.... But the spectator is too likely to be haunted by memories of the later, and much fuller, play, to be completely moved.... It is a pity, too ... the writing is honest and compassionate.*

Theatre Arts, June 1959

Lord Byron's Love Letter

Play in one act.
Written: before 1946. *No professional production.*
Operatic version: Tulane University, New Orleans, Louisiana,
18 Jan. 1955 (score by Raffaello de Banfield; conducted by
Nicola Rescigno; with Patricia Neway as the Grandmother and
Gertrude Ribla as the Spinster); Lyric Th., Chicago, Illinois,
21 Nov. 1955 (conducted by Nicola Rescigno; with Astrid
Varney as the Grandmother and Gertrude Ribla as the
Spinster).
Published (stage version): in *27 Wagons Full of Cotton;* and in
Theatre Vol. VI.

What became of Lord Byron's Love Letter? *Originally it was a tenderly written little fable about an ageing, poverty-stricken old woman who lives in romantic memories of her affair with Lord Byron in her youth. It concluded with a subtle, ironic revelation that changed the relationship between the old woman and her grand-daughter. Although ... small in size, it is written with the rueful poetry and theatrical dexterity that characterizes Mr. Williams's best work.... A little play about some faded people has now become an exuberant Italian opera with lusty singing characters.... Mr. Banfield's score is beautiful, rich, and exhilarating. But it crushes a tenuous libretto.*

Brooks Atkinson, *New York Times,* 19 Jan. 1955

The Strangest Kind of Romance

Play in one act.
Written: before 1946.
First production: Théâtre de Champs Elysées, Paris, 20 Apr. 1960
  (dir. Robert Postec; des. André Acquart; with Paul Chevalier
  as the Little Man and Madelein Parion as the Landlady).
Published: in *27 Wagons Full of Cotton;* and in *Theatre, Vol. VI.*

A lonely, nerve-wracked little man, buffeted by life and landlady, finds warmth only with an independent and symbolic alley cat.

Camino Real

Play in three acts.
Written: as *Ten Blocks on the Camino Real,* 1946.
First New York production: Martin Beck Th., 19 Mar. 1953 (dir.
  Elia Kazan; des. Lemuel Ayers; with Eli Wallach as Kilroy and
  Barbara Baxley as Esmeralda).
First London production: Phoenix Th., 8 Apr. 1957 (dir. Peter
  Hall; with Denholm Elliott as Kilroy and Elisabeth Seal as
  Esmeralda).
Revived: Vivian Beaumont Th., New York, 8 Jan. 1970.
Published: New York: New Directions, 1953; London: Secker
  and Warburg, 1958; in *Four Plays;* and in *Theatre, Vol. II.*
  (The New Directions version differs from the produced version
  in the addition of three characters, a prologue, and several
  scenes, while other scenes are deleted.)

Kilroy is here, Camille is here. Byron, with club foot and blazing eyes, is here. So is Casanova. All are talking of flight . . . while they wait, and engage in cryptic and soulful conversation with one another, a variety of other images erupts around me. A redheaded madame does a broadcast commercial for her brothel, and announces that the moon has generously restored the virginity of her daughter. Silent policemen stalk occasional homosexuals and shoot them down. A man staggers down a concrete staircase and remembers his childhood pony before he dies. As one or another of these not quite human fragments hits the earth, a squad of street-cleaners hoists the departed into a pushcart. . . . At the end,

Kilroy, Camille, and Casanova are led cheerily away by a cosily romantic Don Quixote de la Mancha. Mr. Williams is hopelessly mired in his new love – symbolism. Camino Real *takes place nowhere. . . .*

Walter Kerr, *New York Times*, 20 Mar. 1953

Out of the constantly shifting phantasmagoria we tentatively descry an intention to assert that romantics are the salt of the earth, since they are more conscious of the corruption of society than other people. . . . The intentions are admirable but we suspect that we might miss them altogether if we depended on the spoken word. Mr. Williams in this play goes a long way toward dispensing with language, and such language as he uses tends to collect in patches of 'smog'. . . . It is possible that many of us would prefer to this piece of elevated mystification a good average musical comedy.

The Times, London, 9 Apr. 1957

Some poet has said that a poem should not mean but be. Of course, a play is not a poem, not even a poetic play has quite the same licence as a poem. But to go to *Camino Real* with the inflexible demands of a logician is unfair to both parties. . . . In Philadelphia a young man from a literary periodical saw the play and then cross-examined me about all its dreamlike images. He had made a list of them while he watched the play, and afterward at my hotel he brought out the list and asked me to explain the meaning of each one. I can't deny that I use a lot of these things called symbols but being a self-defensive creature I may say that symbols are nothing but the natural speech of drama. . . . I can't say with any personal conviction that I have written a good play, I only know that I have felt a release in this work which I wanted you to feel in me.

Williams, from the foreword to *Camino Real*, first published in the *New York Times*, 15 Mar. 1953

Williams has been arguing in the *New York Times* that an action like throwing a bag through a window may say more than words. True. And it may be the writer who conceives such an action. Nevertheless, to think of it is very little. The action has meaning only as created by an actor and direction. In *Camino Real*, Williams is not a dramatist but a librettist, a scenario writer. The script when I read it some time ago I disliked. . . . The genuine element in Tennessee Williams had always seemed to me to be his realism: his ability to make eloquent and expressive dialogue out of the real speech of men. . . . *Camino* seemed wholly given over to the non-genuine element . . . [and] doesn't even pretend to realism. The unreal, which formerly crept up on us furtively, now meets us head-on. Whether New York will prefer this I do not know.

Eric Bentley, New Republic, 30 Mar. 1953

When *Camino Real* was first produced in 1953 there were many who found it obscure. Our standards of obscurity, like our standards of obscenity, have escalated since those dark days of theatrical innocence. . . . *Camino Real* is a play that has no story as such, even though it has as many fluttering incidents as an aviary has birds. . . . The play can perhaps best be seen as a symbolic portrait of the American poet . . . of genius lavishly misspent, a defiant play about defeat, a play with the shabby smell of death to it . . . a lovely play, a play of genuinely poetic vision. . . . Seen now from the brink of the 'seventies, *Camino Real* seems oddly prophetic about its author.

Clive Barnes, New York Times, 9 Jan. 1970

If the play, *Camino Real*, was a product being promoted on a TV commercial and I were the spokesman for it, I suppose I would present it in such theatrical terms as these:

'Are you more nervous and anxious than you want people to know?

'Has your public smile come to resemble the grimace of a liontamer in a cage with a suddenly untamed lion, or that of a trapeze performer without a net beneath him . . .?

'And do you have to continue your performance betraying no sign on your face of anxiety in your heart?

'Then here is the right place for you, the Camino Real, its plaza and dried-up fountain, at the end of it. Here is where you won't be lonely alone, bewildered alone, frightened alone, nor desperately brave alone, either.' . . .

What the play says through this unashamed old romanticist, Don Quixote, is just this, 'Life is an unanswered question, but let's still believe in the dignity and importance of the question.'

Williams 'Reflections on a Revival of a Controversial Fantasy',
New York Times, 15 May 1960, reprinted in Where I Live

A Perfect Analysis Given by a Parrot

Play in one act, the dialogue and characters of which appear in
 part in *The Rose Tattoo*, Act I, Scene v.
Written: see *The Rose Tattoo,* below.
First production: Waterfront Playhouse, Key West, 1 May 1970
 (dir. Tennessee Williams).
First New York production: Quaigh Lunchtime Th., 7 June 1976.
Published: Esquire, October 1958; in *Dragon Country;* and in
 Theatre, Vol. VII.

Flora and Bessie, two conventioneer-followers, on a tear in a bar.

The Rose Tattoo

Play in three acts.
Written: beginning in 1948.
First production: Erlanger Th., Chicago, Illinois, 29 Dec. 1950
 (dir. Daniel Mann; des Boris Aronson; with Maureen Stapleton
 as Serafina and Eli Wallach as Alvaro).
First New York production: Martin Beck Th., 3 Feb. 1951 (dir.
 Daniel Mann; des. Boris Aronson; with Maureen Stapleton as
 Serafina and Eli Wallach as Alvaro).
First English productions: New Shakespeare Theatrical Club,
 Liverpool, 4 Nov. 1958; New Th., London, 15 Jan. 1959 (dir.
 Sam Wanamaker; with Lea Padovani as Serafina and Sam
 Wanamaker as Alvaro).
Revived: City Center Th., New York City, 20 Oct. 1966; Billy
 Rose Th., New York City, 9 Nov. 1966.
Film version: Paramount, 1955 (dir. Daniel Mann).
Published: New York: New Directions, 1951; London: Secker
 and Warburg, 1954; in *Five Plays;* and in *Theatre, Vol. II.*

*Tennessee Williams specializes in – he would perhaps like to
think himself the poet of – the sexual rage, displayed here in a
Sicilian peasant glorying in the prowess of her husband, who
claims to be a baron and is a lorry-driver smuggling dope beneath
his loads of bananas. . . . When her husband is shot, [this woman]
isolates herself for three years in her grief, produces stigmata on
her breast, lets herself degenerate into a slattern, reveres the ashes*

*of her dead husband in her private shrine, and locks her daughter
in a room without any clothes because she has dated a sailor. . . .
Because [Williams] has a great theatrical flair he externalizes
[abberations] in roles which are blown up and then, if acted full
out, give the momentary illusion of something grander, larger,
more universal, aimed in fact at the tragic dimension. . . .*

T.C. Worsley, *New Statesman*, 24 Jan. 1959

We don't know that we'll get a better play all season. A bird in
hand is worth two at the billboards. . . . I've used the phrase 'bird
in hand' deliberately, by the way, because that is what the play is
like: it pecks, flutters, pulses with funny panic, all but bursts with
the heat and strain of being contained.

Walter Kerr, *New York Times*, 20 Nov. 1966

The Rose Tattoo is the Dionysian element in human life, its
mystery, its beauty, its significance. . . . It is the *rosa mystica*, the
light on the bare golden flesh of a god whose back is turned to us
or whose face is covered . . . it is the desire of an artist to work in
new forms, however awkwardly at first, to break down barriers of
what he has done before and what others have done better before
and after and to crash, perhaps fatally, into some area that the
bell-harness and rope would like to forbid him. . . . It may seem
curious that I have chosen a woman to be the main protagonist
of a play on such a theme. But in the blind and frenzied efforts
of the widow, Serafina, to comprehend the mysteries of her dead
husband, we sense and learn more about him than would have
been possible through direct observation of the living man, the
Dionysus himself. Dionysus, being mystery, is never seen clearly.
He can not be confined to memory nor an urn, nor the conven-
tions and proprieties of a plump little seamstress who wanted to
fortify her happiness with the respect of the community.

Williams, *Vogue*, 15 March 1951, reprinted in *Where I Live*

Talk to Me Like the Rain and Let Me Listen

Play in one act.
Written: c.1950.
First production: White Barn Th., Westport, Connecticut, 26 July 1958.
Revived: in *Three by Tennessee,* Lolly's Th. Club, New York City, 6 Dec. 1973 (dir. Dick Garfield and Cindy Kaplans).
Television production: PBS-TV, 3 Dec. 1970 (dir. Glenn Jordan; with Lois Smith as the Woman and William Mixon as the Man).
Published: in *27 Wagons Full of Cotton* (1953, 1966 editions).

Man rises from a debauch and reaches for Woman, who chants to him her perfect fantasy of seaside peace and quiet.

Eccentricities of a Nightingale

Play in three acts.
Written: 1951, as a revised version of *Summer and Smoke* (see p. 23).
First productions: Tappan Zee Playhouse, Nyack, New York, 25 June 1964; Theater Club, Washington, D.C., 20 Apr. 1966 (dir. Darcy Marlin-Jones; with Melinda Miller as Alma and Raymond Thorne as John).
First English production: Yvonne Arnaud Th., Guildford, Oct. 1967.
Revived: Studio Arena Th., Buffalo, N.Y., 8 October 1976; Morosco Th., New York City, 23 Nov. 1976; Long Beach Theatre Festival, California, 14 Feb. 1979.
Television production: PBS-TV, 16 June 1976 (with Blythe Danner as Alma and Frank Langella as John).
Published: New York: New Directions, 1964; and in *Theatre, Vol. II.*

The new work effectively knocks Summer and Smoke *off the map, except as a literary curiosity – the old play contrasted man's soul and his body, and pointed out, with fairly heavy symbolism, the dangers of dividing the two. The new play is a straightforward conflict of two people — one hot and one cold, a woman at base nervously confident, and a man at base confidently nervous . . . far more complex and credible than their counterparts in the earlier plays, and the resolution of their conflict is far neater and more satisfying.*

Clive Barnes, *New York Times,* 24 Nov. 1976

Sweet Bird of Youth

Play in two acts.
Written: as a revised version of *The Enemy — Time* (published in *Theatre,* March 1959), 1952.
First production: Studio M Playhouse, Coral Gables, Florida, 16 Apr. 1956 (dir. and des. George Keathley; with Alan Mixon as Phil and Margrit Wyler as Princess).
First New York production: Martin Beck Th., 10 Mar. 1959 (dir. Elia Kazan; des. Jo Mielziner and Anna Hill Johnstone; with Paul Newman as Chance Wayne and Geraldine Page as Princess).
First English production: Experimental Club, Manchester, Feb. 1964.
Revived: Civic Playhouse, Los Angeles, California, 1 Nov. 1961; Palace, Watford, 14 Nov. 1968 (dir. Giles Havergal; with Christopher Gable as Chance Wayne and Vivien Merchant as Princess); Kennedy Center, Washington, D.C., 9 Oct. 1975; Brooklyn Academy of Music, Brooklyn, New York, 3 Dec. 1975; Harkness Th., 29 Dec. 1975.
Film version: Metro-Goldwyn-Mayer, 1962 (dir. Richard Brooks).
Published: London: Penguin, 1962; New York: New Directions, 1959; in *Esquire,* April 1957; and in *Theatre, Vol. IV.*

Chance Wayne is an average small-town boy . . . at the age of seventeen he has an idyllic affair with a girl of fifteen. But because he is poor, the girl's father — political boss of the town — calls an abrupt halt to the romance. The boy goes to New York in the hope of becoming enough of a big shot as an actor to impress the folks back home. . . . He is drafted for the Korean war. . . . On his release from the Navy one of his jobs is that of masseur at a Florida beach resort. He earns money on the side as a gigolo. One of the women he encounters is a fading movie star in flight from impending failure. . . . Chance Wayne brings her back to his home town. He clings to this woman — whose whore he becomes — because he plans to make her the key to a Hollywood career for himself. . . . At some point before these latter events, Chance had resumed his affair with the girl who is his true love. Sometime during his career as a gigolo he had contracted a venereal disease and had unknowingly infected his beloved. Her father has her undergo an operation which renders her sterile. The girl bids the boy — still ignorant of what has happened — to leave town for good lest her father have him killed. . . . The boy virtually invites the castration with which he has been threatened. . . .

Williams does not ask us to forgive the boy, but the whole play suggests that he is sufficiently typical to induce us to share some kinship with him. . . . Taken literally, Chance Wayne is an atrocity. He is not a real person but a figment of Williams's commanding sentiment. . . . What we suspect in *Sweet Bird of Youth* is that Williams has become immobilized in his ideology; that it has not been refreshed either by any new experience or by mature thought. He has only become much bolder. The result is that we feel in this play an invested sentimentality and a wilful stress which produce more ugliness than lyricism or credence.

Harold Clurman, *The Nation*, 28 Mar. 1959

Still possessed of demons, Mr. Williams is not revenging himself on anyone this time . . . it is a play that ranges wide through the lower depths, touching on political violence, as well as diseases of mind and body. But it has the spontaneity of an improvisation. Nothing seems to be planned. . . . [Mr. Williams] seems to have made some sort of peace with himself. *Sweet Bird of Youth* is one of his finest dramas.

Brooks Atkinson, *New York Times*, 11 Mar. 1959

Welcomed by some as less formidable than several of his earlier pieces . . . it would appear that the only mature point of view to bring to these characters is that of comedy with comedy's detachment and mockery — a mockery these 'monsters' richly deserve, as does the world of cheap values — the charlatanry, cheap success, vainglory, dog-eat-dog motivation, and alternating hypocrisy and cynicism variously exemplified in their conduct and confessions.

John Gassner, *Educational Theatre Journal*, May 1959

In *Sweet Bird of Youth,* Tennessee Williams seems less concerned with dramatic verisimilitude than with communicating some hazy notions about such disparate items as Sex, Youth, Time, Corruption, Purity, Castration, Politics and the South. . . . Cavorting through the forest of his own unconscious, Williams has taken to playing hide-and-go-seek with reality in a manner which he does not always control. *Sweet Bird of Youth* . . . frequently looks less like art than like some kind of confession and apology. . . . About to be castrated, the play's hero, Chance Wayne, turns to the audience to ask for 'the recognition of me in you, and the enemy, time, in us all!' Since Chance has had about as much universality as a character in an animated cartoon, to regard his experience as an illuminating reflection of the human condition is a notion which borders on the grotesque.

Robert Brustein, *Hudson Review,* Summer 1959

Something Unspoken

Play in one act.
Written: before 1953.
First production: Lakeside Summer Th., Lake Hopatcong, New Jersey, 22 June 1955 (dir. Herbert Machiz; des. Paul Georges, Jack Haupman; with Patricia Ripley as Cornelia and Hortense Alden as Grace).
First New York production: with *Suddenly Last Summer,* as *Garden District,* York Th., 7 Feb. 1958 (dir. Herbert Machiz; des. Robert Soule and Stanley Simmons; with Eleanor Phelps as Cornelia Scott and Hortense Alden as Grace Lancaster).
First London production: with *Suddenly Last Summer,* as *Garden District,* Arts Th., 16 Sept. 1958 (dir. Herbert Machiz; with Beryl Measor as Cornelia Scott and Beatrix Lehmann as Grace Lancaster).
Revived: Lolly's Th. Club, 6 Dec. 1973 (dir. Dick Garfield and Cindy Kaplans).
Published: London: Secker and Warburg, 1959, with *Suddenly Last Summer;* in *27 Wagons Full of Cotton* (1953 edition, 1966 edition); in *Five plays;* and in *Theatre, Vol. VII.*

A crucial afternoon in the lives of two spinsters: Cornelia, the imperious Daughter of the Confederacy, and Grace, her fragile little secretary, who compares herself bitterly to a cobweb and refuses to discuss what has to remain unspoken.

Senso/The Wanton Countess

Screenplay.
Written: 1953.
Produced: Lux, 1954 (dir. Luchino Visconti).

A novel-like depiction of an ill-fated illicit romance intertwined with a momentous chapter in Italy's fight for freedom from the Austrians, it is an obvious, rudimentary operatic approach to amour and an illustration of history that is likely to be fuzzy to anyone but a student of Garibaldi's 1866 campaign around Venice and Verona.

A.H. Weiler, *New York Times,* 9 July 1968

Later, when I did the screenplay for *Senso,* Luchino Visconti used his old standby . . . to rewrite my script and when I finally saw *that* one, only one scene of mine was left — a scene in a bedroom with two people waking up in a bed. There was a line that went, 'There's always a sound in a room when you wake', and Visconti had a fly buzzing around. Of course, that's not what I meant at all. When I wake up I always start belching.

Williams, interviewed by Rex Reed, *Esquire,* September 1971

Three Players of a Summer Game

Play in one act.
Written: 1954.
First production: White Barn Th., Westport, Connecticut, 19 July 1955. *Unpublished.*

Based on the short story from which Cat on a Hot Tin Roof *was developed,* Three Players *bears very little resemblance to* Cat *in either incarnation, except for the presence of Brick, an alcoholic husband, and Margaret, his wife. The story is told by a friend of their child, Mary Louise, and the 'summer game' is croquet.*

Cat on a Hot Tin Roof

Play in three acts.

Written: 1955, adapted from the same short story as *Three
   Players of a Summer Game* (see p. 39).

First New York production: Morosco Th., 24 Mar. 1955 (dir.
   Elia Kazan; des. Jo Mielziner and Lucinda Ballard; with
   Barbara Bel Geddes as Margaret, Ben Gazzara as Brick, and
   Burl Ives as Big Daddy).

First London production: Comedy Th., 30 Jan. 1958 (dir. Peter
   Hall; with Kim Stanley as Maggie, Paul Massie as Brick, and
   Leo McKern as Big Daddy.)

Revived: American Shakespeare Th., Stratford, Connecticut, 10
   July 1974; ANTA Th., New York, 24 Sept. 1975; Mark Taper
   Forum, Los Angeles, 11 Aug. 1983.

Film version: Metro-Goldwyn-Mayer, 1958 (dir. Richard Brooks).

Television production: NBC-TV, 1976.

Published: New York: New Directions, 1955; London: Secker
   and Warburg, 1956; in *Five Plays;* and in *Theatre, Vol. III.*

---

*In a dimly-lit, significantly shuttered bed-sitting room on a
Mississippi plantation, a young and handsome athlete hobbles
about on crutches, heads for his private bar with purposeful
regularity, and refuses to sleep with his wife. He had had, in his
life, one profound friendship: with a fellow football player. The
friend is now dead – dead of drink – and this bitter and sodden
Tennessee Williams hero is sure of just one thing. The descent of
his friend, and his own as well, began with a half-uttered suspicion
on the part of his wife – a suspicion that the close relationship of
the two men was unnatural. . . . The young man's parents nag and
scratch at him in greedy hope of an heir. . . .*

This play at the Morosco stretches this tormented soul taut on
the rack and then claws at his open 'sores'. . . . We never quite
penetrate Brick's own facade, know or share his precise feelings. . . .
in *Cat on a Hot Tin Roof* you will believe every word that is unspoken; you may still long for some that seem not be spoken. . . .
This is, I think, a flaw in the work. It should not keep you from
seeing it. Mr. Williams is the man of our time who comes closest
to hurling the actual blood and bone of life onto the stage; he is
also the man whose prose comes closest to being an incisive

natural poetry.
Walter Kerr, *New York Herald-Tribune,* 25 Mar. 1955

Again, Mr. Williams is discussing some people of the Mississippi Delta, which he knows well ... but this time, Mr. Williams has broken free from the formula ... that has hovered around the edges of his plays. ... To say that it is the drama of people who refuse to face the truth of life is to suggest a whole school of problem dramatists ... [but] it seems not to have been written. It is the quintessence of life. It is the basic truth ... a delicately wrought exercise in human communications ... Mr. Williams' finest drama. It faces and speaks the truth.
Brooks Atkinson, *New York Times,* 25 Mar. 1955

In a way, Mr. Williams has stacked his cards a little too obviously, since his corrupted idealist is as picturesque and charming a figure as any the theatre has recently produced, and his bore isn't much more than a standard low-comedy caricature. There is never any question about the old man's real emotional commitment, and I should say that in this particular, too much legitimate dramatic suspense may have been sacrificed for a kind of self-conscious literary integrity. Mr. Williams, that is, has in general scornfully declined to write anything that could possibly be defined as a 'commercial' play. ... There are villains, but they are far too ludicrous to concern anybody much. If you really care about who gets the ten million dollars and the twenty-eight thousand acres of the most fertile land this side of the Nile, the Morosco is not the theatre you're looking for.
Wolcott Gibbs, *New Yorker,* 2 Apr. 1955

Mr. Tennessee Williams gives the impression that he has prepared and brought to the boiling point a special serum made up of greed, sexual frustration, sexual longing, and sexual uncertainty, and has injected it into his leading characters. ... The tooth-and-nail conflicts within the arena are exciting to watch ... but when it is over we feel no concern for anybody's soul. We calmly recall the gameness of one fighting animal under punishment and the savagery of the other when cornered.
The Times, London, 31 Jan. 1958

41

The subject of Brick's sexual confusion is no longer the sensation that it once was, so that the real theme of the play — the general mendacity of our society — is more clearly seen. Watergate may have been helpful to *Cat*.

New York Times, 21 December 1975

The bird that I hope to catch in the net of this play is not the solution of one man's psychological problem. I'm trying to catch the true quality of experience in a group of people, that cloudy, flickering, evanescent — fiercely charged! — interplay of live human beings in the thundercloud of a common crisis.

Williams, stage directions to *Cat*, Act II

People are always asking me which is my favourite among the plays I have written, the number of which eludes my recollection, and I either say to them 'always the latest' or I succumb to my instinct for the truth and say, 'I suppose it must be the published version of *Cat on a Hot Tin Roof*'. That play comes closest to being both a work of art and a work of craft. . . . I believe that in *Cat* I reached beyond myself, in the second act, to a kind of crude eloquence of expression in Big Daddy that I have managed to give no other character of my creation.

Williams, *Memoirs*, p. 168

Orpheus Descending

Play in three acts.
Written: as a revised version of *Battle of Angels* (see page 14).
First New York production: Martin Beck Th., 21 Mar. 1957 (dir. Harold Clurman; des. Boris Aronson, Lucinda Ballard, and Feder; with Cliff Robertson as Val Xavier and Maureen Stapleton as Lady Torrance).
First London production: Royal Court Th., 14 May 1959 (dir. Tony Richardson; with Gary Cockrell as Val and Isa Miranda as Lady Torrance).
Revived: Circle Th., New York City, 3 Nov. 1974.
Film version: as *The Fugitive Kind*, 1960.
Published: New York: New Directions, 1958; London: Secker and Warburg, 1958; in *Five Plays;* and in *Theatre, Vol. III*.

*It has all Mr. Williams's ingredients in one dish: his early roman-
ticism and later symbolism, the poeticisms of his* Rose Tattoo
*period, and his later sweatshirt realism. It has, too, all the usual
conflicts: decadence and idealism, youth and age, innocence and
corruption. And it keeps them up for over three hours. . . . A
footloose guitar player . . . wanders into a decadent but symbolic Southern township, which, as Mr. Williams justifiably
suggests, is the closest thing imaginable to hell on earth. He resists
the advances of a wistful, young nymphomaniac . . . but falls for
an ageing Eurydice. . . . She is the daughter of another wandering
minstrel, who had once run a bacchic clip-joint until he was burnt
out and killed by the KKK for lack of discrimination (racial). The
daughter discovers that her ailing husband has led the attack and
she is determined to see him done for. Orpheus waits with her too
long and is torn apart. . . .*

No doubt all the best artists are in some degree symbolic. But
symbols do their work without being continually jollied along by
their creator. Mr. Williams, alas, can't leave them alone. He is
forever harping on them, explaining them, as though he had read,
and, which is worse, believed his most highflown interpreters. . . .
It is in his values that he goes most haywire. His characters inhabit
an A.A. Milne world where 'the cold's so cold and the hot's so
hot' – no middle ground between innocence and corruption. . . .
Fundamentally, there is little difference between the moral world
of *Orpheus Descending* and that of *Peter Pan,* except that Mr.
Williams's creed is that of Apartness. . . .

A. Alvarez, *New Statesman,* 23 May 1959

This one is less baleful than some of the worlds he has put together
recently. . . . *Orpheus Descending* is one of Mr. Williams's plea-
santest plays, with characters determined to free themselves from
corruption. . . . Mr. Williams's style of writing elliptically is a
fundamental part of his gift. He does not attack his scenes head-
on. They grow out of improvisations. But it seems to this play-
goer that Mr. Williams has his story less thoroughly under control
this time, and his allusive style has a less sturdy foundation. . . .
Orpheus is not sure of his direction.

Brooks Atkinson, *New York Times,* 22 Mar. 1957

43

The drama is rather closer to the dark, indolent, keening lyricism of Mr. Williams's poems and stories than it is to the brilliant tangibilities of wit and observation which stud *A Streetcar Named Desire* and *The Glass Menagerie*. Tragedy brings into collision the person and the cosmos, and in *Orpheus Descending* the two parts of this equation never come into balance. Mr. Williams's Orphic hero, having rejected any traffic in personal or social commitment, cannot enter into experience; he is a lyric rather than a dramatic figure. And since his destiny never assumes the rhythm of inevitability, the handing of him over to death — a literal throwing to the bloodhounds — seems a wanton stroke by the playwright, an outrage to human feeling, and a mean trapping of the audience into emotions from which it cannot escape.

Richard Hayes, *The Commonweal*, 26 Apr. 1957

Suddenly Last Summer

Play in one act.

First New York production: with *Something Unspoken,* as *Garden District,* York Th., 7 Jan. 1958 (dir. Herbert Machiz; des. Robert Soule, Stanley Simmons, and Lee Watson; with Anne Meacham as Catherine Holly and Hortense Alden as Mrs. Venable).

First London production: Arts Th., 16 Sept. 1958 (dir. Herbert Machiz; with Patricia Neal as Catherine Holly and Beatrix Lehmann as Mrs. Venable).

Revived: Master Th., New York, 30 Oct. 1964; Greene Street Th., Key West, Florida, Apr. 1976.

Film version: Columbia Pictures, 1959 (dir. Joseph Mankiewicz, with screenplay by Williams).

Published: Norfolk, Ct: New Directions, 1958; London: Secker and Warburg, 1959; in *Five Plays;* and in *Theatre, Vol. III.*

While Suddenly Last Summer *... is in my opinion an impressive and genuinely shocking play, it is certainly not without its odd, unsettling air of self-parody. ... The story ... is concerned with the bloodcurdling manner in which a poet is said to have met his death. ... Like Dorian Gray ... this man was substantially immune to the ravages of vice. ... [His mother and a cousin] were, in their separate ways, strongly and abnormally attracted to* *him, and both are convinced that he was a genius. . . . The struggle between them has an intermittent dark eloquence and a sustained chilling ferocity that, for the most part, take it successfully out of absurdity and into pure horror. . . . I know of no playwright except Mr. Williams who would deliberately threaten an audience with the performance of a prefrontal lobotomy (the mother's bleakly efficient prescription for keeping her rival's mouth shut) or who could invent a story of quite such lurid perversity (a form of cannibalism gets into it, if you care) that the young woman tells about her doomed cousin. . . . Considering all its manifestations, Mr. Williams's talent is one of the most singular of our time. You may not always be quite easy in its presence, but it is practically impossible to remain indifferent to it. . . .*

Wolcott Gibbs, *New Yorker,* 18 January 1958

When Big Daddy in *Cat on a Hot Tin Roof* asks his son, Brick, why he drinks, the answer, teasingly withheld until another drink is offered, finally comes forth as DISGUST, in large type. Big Daddy, exasperated, shouts back in bold type DISGUST WITH WHAT? Of course, Brick isn't truly suffering from disgust at all, but from a wan, sexappealy, soaking, localcolour *disenchantment*. . . . 'Stressing false values' is a favourite revelation among playwrights, even though the recognition of this condition is seldom seen in real life. Tennessee Williams goes in for revelation of another sort. It is not spiritual or moral, but frankly sexual, like a sudden undressing. At the final curtain in a Williams play everyone is running about with his clothes off. . . . *Suddenly Last Summer* . . . is for the deeply jaded, the hung-over. Williams has after all given us everything, and here, desperate at last, he offers up a dish of cannibalism . . . but the tribal world is peopled with old friends.

Elizabeth Hardwick, *Partisan Review,* Spring 1958

For Mr. Tennessee Williams the world is a place in which we become aware of others only in so far as they stimulate our awareness of ourselves; there can be no intimacy, for intimacy is the act of awarding identity to another, and we tolerate the world only as an extension of ourselves, the children. There is no love, there is use, and endless feeding of the emotions without risk or involvement; other people simply satisfy an appetite, the world is a restaurant. 'Here', in short, 'be cannibals'. . . . Mr. Williams is a doggedly minor artist, unable to distinguish between the usual and the odd. We *know* the world is not cannibalistic, and he does not, for he has found cannibalism or its equivalent in odd corners and assumes it to be universal. His attitude to the world? Regret, but also fascination; for on the map he draws for us, the words 'Here be cannibals' read as much like an invitation to the feast as a warning.

Robert Robinson, *New Statesman*, 27 Sept. 1958

It matters less that noisomely misanthropic symbols keep recurring in his work than that they nowhere seem purgative. Playwright Williams, who is undergoing analysis, recently said that *Suddenly* is a final fling at violence.

Time, 20 Jan. 1958

Period of Adjustment

Play in three acts.
Written: 1957-58.
First production: Cocoanut Grove Playhouse, Miami, Florida, 29 Dec. 1958 (dir. Williams and Owen Phillips).
First New York production: Helen Hayes Th., 10 Nov. 1960 (dir. George Roy Hill; des. Jo Mielziner and Patricia Zipprodt; with James Daly as Ralph Bates, Barbara Baxley as Isabel Haverstick, and Robert Webber as George Haverstick).
First London production: Royal Court Th., 13 June 1962, trans. to Wyndhams Th., 10 July 1962 (dir. by Roger Graef; with Bernard Braden as Ralph Bates, Collin Wincox as Isabel Haverstick, and Neill McGallum as George).
Film version: Metro-Goldwyn-Mayer, 1962 (dir. George Roy Hill, screenplay by Isobel Lennart).
Published: in *Esquire,* December 1960; New York: New Directions, 1960; London: Secker and Warburg, 1961; and in *Theatre, Vol. IV.*

A domestic comedy dealing with one inept and one jaded couple and a disastrous mutual honeymoon.

The most obvious fact about *Period of Adjustment* is that Tennessee Williams has proved with it that he can write an optimistic comedy. The obvious answer to this is that so can other playwrights. . . . He has also demonstrated . . . that he can write 'wholesomely', to which I can only add that I prefer his 'decadence' to his 'health'. There have been legions of health-minded playwrights available to the American theatre, but I haven't noticed they have done much for our stage. . . .

John Gassner, *Educational Theatre Journal,* March 1961

This is the kind of study in human relations they know how to make in Hollywood, it is put on and played in the proper fashion: much better, we would say, than it was on the Broadway stage.

Bosley Crowther, *New York Times,* 1 Nov. 1962, on the film version

[*Period of Adjustment*] is a distinct hit — Williams's first real box-office success in England. . . . It is not the production in London which has turned the play into a success: it is the audience. The audience provides the play's comment. The English stage has latterly become tougher and rougher, its public more eager to see the depiction of working-class people and environments — and provincial ones at that — a milieu that was rare in the West End theatre before 1956. . . . In *Period of Adjustment,* Williams pokes fun at the sexual timidity, frustration, psychic impotence, gingerliness of the average (Puritan) American. . . . The English can appreciate this, for, in somewhat different fashion, but even more widely and acutely, they are similarly affected. . . . Frank, open discussion and presentation of sexual impulses in public places like the theatre is still sketchy. The bonds are about to burst. . . . This breakthrough will at first probably take the form of good-humoured comedies like *Period of Adjustment,* in which the Londoners can have their sexual cake, and at the same time laugh it off. . . .

Harold Clurman, *The Nation,* 11 Aug. 1962

The Night of the Iguana

Play in three acts.

First New York production: Royale Th., 29 Dec. 1961 (dir. Frank Corsaro; with Bette Davis as Maxine Faulk and Patrick O'Neal as Rev. T. Lawrence Shannon).

First London production: Ashcroft Th., Croydon, Feb. 1965, trans. to Savoy Th., 24 Mar. 1965 (dir. Philip Wiseman;

des. Peter Farmer; with Vanda Godsell as Maxine Faulk and
Mark Eden as Shannon).

Revived: Circle in the Square, New York City, 16 Dec. 1976.

Film version: Metro-Goldwyn-Mayer/Seven Arts, 1964 (dir.
John Huston).

Published: in *Esquire,* Feb. 1962; New York: New Directions,
1962; London: Secker and Warburg, 1963; and in *Theatre,
Vol. IV.*

---

*'The going to pieces of T. Lawrence Shannon', a phrase from the
play, might be its more appropriate title, for it focuses mainly on
the degradation and breakdown of its central character, a crapu-
lous and slightly psychotic Episcopalian minister . . . thrown out
of his church for 'fornication and heresy'. . . . Shannon now con-
ducts guided tours in Mexico, sleeping with underage girls, coping
with hysterical female Baptists. . . . Other characters brush by this
broken heretic, and they hardly connect with him, except to
uncover his psycho-sexual history and expose their own: the
patrona of the hotel, a hearty lecherous widow . . . out of Sweet
Bird of Youth; Hannah Jelkes, a virgin spinster with a compassionate nature, out of Summer and Smoke; and Nonno, her
father, a 97-year-old poet – deaf, cackling and comatose – out of
Krapp's Last Tape. The substance of the play is the exchange, by
Hannah and Shannon, of mutual confidences about their sexual
failures, while the patrona shoots him hot glances and the poet
labours to complete his last poem. . . .*

The materials, while resolved without sensationalism or sentiment, are all perfectly familiar. . . . A rich atmosphere, a series of
languid scenes, and some interesting character sketches are more
than Williams has offered us in some time, but they are still not
enough to sustain an interest through a full evening. . . . Let us
put down *The Night of the Iguana* as another of his innumerable
exercises in marking time.

Robert Brustein, *New Republic,* 22 Jan. 1962

Sometimes I wonder if the trouble with Tennessee Williams isn't
simply the lack of a geographical term: a name for that sub-
tropical empire Napoleon III sent Maximilian and Carlotta to

carve out round the Gulf of Mexico. Increasingly it becomes apparent that events down there — Huey Long, the Cuban invasion from Florida, the Kennedy assassination itself — belong not to the familiar American patterns, but to a hotter, wilder subcivilization, more Latin than Yankee. To call it the South won't answer; the overtones of Margaret Mitchell gentility are wrong; even Faulkner seems a world away. The central figure of Williams's geography is an undefined frontier land yielding swampily, imperceptibly to shallow sea, moss garden to jungle.... It is a real confusion; if the map admitted it, would Williams be forced to such overwrought lengths to establish it as a region of the mind?...

The Night of the Iguana ... marks another stage in his curious decay of structural grasp. I can think of no other dramatist whose career has progressed so palpably from assurance to uncertainty, from mastery of theatrical technique to apprentice fumbling....

Ronald Bryden, *New Statesman*, 2 April 1965

The Milk Train Doesn't Stop Here Anymore

Play in six scenes.
Written: beginning in 1959.
First production: Festival of Two Worlds, Spoleto, Italy, 11 July 1962.
First New York production: Morosco Th., 16 Jan. 1963 (dir. Herbert Machiz; with Hermione Baddeley as Mrs. Goforth).
First London production: Tower Th., Nov. 1968 (dir. Edgar Davies; with Sara Randall as Mrs. Goforth).
Revived: Brooks Atkinson Th., New York City, 1 Jan. 1964; Encore Th., San Francisco, California, 23 July 1965.
Film version: as *Boom!,* Limites/Word Film Services, Universal, 1968 (dir. Joseph Losey; with Tallulah Bankhead as Goforth and Tab Hunter as Chris Flanders).
Published: New York: New Directions, 1964; London: Secker and Warburg, 1964; and in *Theatre, Vol. V.*

We are not far from Capri, in Mrs. Goforth's splendid villa. Mrs. Goforth, among husbands who were merely rich, has embedded one who was also beautiful. Picture her feelings, therefore, when a strange young man in lederhosen *walks up the path, in answer to a forgotten invitation. He is exactly like the beautiful husband, but poorer, and Mrs. Goforth is determined to get him. . . . And thereafter the play becomes totally inexplicable . . . [and] seems to have been concocted by several hands, some of them extremely adolescent. Who, precisely, is the stranger? . . . He appears to have strayed out of a play by T.S. Eliot. And who on earth is Mrs. Goforth? At one moment she is straight from a 1920s revue, and wheezily amusing at that; at the next she is a distraught figure aspiring to tragedy. . . . It is a tribute to the trouble taken all round . . . that one is left with the wish to pay a second visit in order to see how Mrs. Goforth is faring.*

Stanley Richards, *Theatre Arts*, Feb. 1963

This fiasco . . . cannot but serve as a reminder that silk purses simply cannot be made out of sow's ears no matter how fine the stitching. The sow's ear in this case is the appalling female on whom the author wasted his talent and his public's patience. . . . As elsewhere, Mr. Williams wavered between his flair for naturalism and his aspirations toward symbolic poetry, and in *The Milk Train* he appeared to have been mired by the former and confused by the latter.

John Gassner, *Educational Theatre Journal*, Mar. 1964

Boom! is a comedy about death. Hermione Baddeley did it on stage as *Milk Train* and she was beautiful. She broke my heart. But that's the problem with me. Everybody breaks my heart.

Williams, interviewed by Arthur Bell, *Village Voice*, 24 Feb. 1972

If you write a play with a very strong female role, such as Flora Goforth of *The Milk Train Doesn't Stop Here Anymore,* it is likely to surface repeatedly, since female stars of a certain age have a rough time finding vehicles suitable to their talents, personalities, and public images. To call *Milk Train* a vehicle is somewhat unfair to it. In that play — really only successful, scriptwise, as the movie *Boom!* — I was fanatically obsessed with trying to say certain things. It was a work of art manqué. . . . *Milk Train* appears to be on a side track shunted there, I'm afraid, by the excessively beauteous Goforth of Liz Taylor in *Boom!* — it remains a marvellous vehicle for an equally marvellous female star, and I don't mean the planet Venus.

Williams, Memoirs, p. 198, 201

I Can't Imagine Tomorrow

Play in one act.
First production: Bar Harbor, Maine, 1971.
Television production: PBS-TV, 3 Dec. 1970 (dir. Glenn Jordan; with Kim Stanley as One, William Redfield as Two).
Published: in *Esquire,* March 1966; in *Dragon Country;* and in *Theatre, Vol. VII.*

In Tomorrow *there are only two characters . . . 'each is the only friend of the other'. The male, a teacher, is now almost totally unable to speak. The two meet every evening to play cards and watch television. Everything is reduced to nothing, and there is nothing left but death. It is a reflection of Tennessee's mood at his lowest point during the crack-up.*

Williams and Mead, Tennessee Williams, p. 301

Slapstick Tragedy

Double-bill of one-act plays comprising:

The Gnädiges Fräulein
Play in one act.
First New York production: with *The Mutilated* as *Slapstick Tragedy,* Longacre Th., 22 Feb. 1966 (dir. Alan Schneider; des. Ming Cho Lee, Noel Taylor, and Martin Aronstein; with Kate Reid as Molly, Margaret Leighton as the Fraulein, and Zoe Caldwell as Polly); *revised version* (as *The Latter Days of a Celebrated Soubrette*): Central Arts Cabaret Th., 16 May 1974 (dir. Luis Lopez-Cepero; with Anne Meacham as the Fraulein, Robert Frink as Molly, and William Pritz as Polly).
Published: in *Esquire,* August 1965; in *Dragon Country;* and in *Theatre, Vol. VII.*

The Mutilated
Play in one act.
First New York production: with *The Gnädiges Fräulein* as

Slapstick Tragedy, Longacre Th., 22 Feb. 1966 (dir. Alan
Schneider; des. Ming Cho Lee; with Margaret Leighton as
Trinket and Kate Reid as Celeste).
Published: New York: Dramatists Play Service, 1967; in
Dragon Country; and in *Theatre, Vol. VII.*

The plays are melancholy but masked avowals. The first, called
The Mutilated, *might be described as a freakish Christmas Carol.
Two whores – the first has had one of her breasts removed, the
other has just been released from a short-term jail sentence for
shoplifting – become reconciled in wretched companionship one
Christmas Eve. . . . As in certain of his former plays, Williams in*
The Mutilated *reveals his compassion – more, his sense of identi-
fication – with the insulted and the injured, the misfits and the
maimed. But while the earlier plays were soft in sentiment,* The
Mutilated *is savage. Its 'slapstick' consists of deliberate bitchi-
ness . . . the intention is to make us see that the two women, one
stupidly infantile, the other horribly stricken with shame at her
affliction, are as absurd as they are pitiable. Williams refuses to
gush over them; they are meant to be both grotesque and ridicu-
lous, and these qualities themselves are to lend the women all the
commiseration they need to make them kin to us. . . .*

The second . . . The Gnädiges Fräulein *is more interesting . . . a
stylized essay in farcical fantasy altogether new for Williams. . . .
The Fräulein earns her keep in a Godforsaken boarding house at
the seaboard of the southernmost part of our States by fighting
to catch fish in the waters whipped by the hurricanes which
harass the place. The difficulty of bringing in the fish (prestige,
status, success) is compounded by the jealousy and competition
of a bird of prey, the Cocaloony. . . . However we interpret this
nightmare, it is written in an odd but effective mixture of gallows
humour and Rabelaisian zest. . . . Though I was able to appreciate
the style I could not bring myself to smile. I was too conscious
that its author was in pain. . . .*

Harold Clurman, The Nation, 14 Mar. 1966

Kingdom of Earth/
Seven Descents of Myrtle

Play in two acts.
Written: 1966-67.
First New York production: as *Seven Descents of Myrtle,* Ethel
    Barrymore Th., 27 Mar. 1968 (dir. Jose Quintero; des. Jo
    Mielziner and Jane Greenwood; with Harry Guardino as
    Chicken, Brian Bedford as Lot, and Estelle Parsons as Myrtle).
First London production: as *Kingdom of Earth,* New Vic Th.,
    14 Feb. 1978 (dir. Mike Newell; des. John Elvery; with Pete
    Postlethwaite as Chicken, Jonathan Kent as Lot, and Gillian
    Borge as Myrtle).
Revived: as *Kingdom of Earth,* McCarter Th. Company,
    Princeton, New Jersey, 11 Mar. 1975.
Film version: as *Last of the Mobile Hot Shots* (*Blood Kin* for
    European release), Warner Brothers/Seven Arts, 1964 (dir.
    Sidney Lumet).
Published: in *Esquire,* Feb. 1967; New York: New Directions,
    1968; and in *Theatre, Vol. V.*

*Tennessee Williams's flop about a dying transvestite who marries
a Southern birdbrain on a TV show to keep his Negro half-brother
from inheriting the family plantation bears no resemblance to any
human beings living or dead who ever inhabited Uncle Remus
country or anywhere else.*

Rex Reed, *Holiday,* Mar. 1970

Time was when Tennessee Williams wrote plays, but nowadays he
seems to prefer to write characters. . . . The suspicion arises that
Mr. Williams is writing a parody of Mr. Williams, a suspicion fanned
by a series of extraordinarily funny jokes. . . . The play's message is
summed up with Chicken's philosophy that life is fine if you can
come home from work and find the right woman waiting on the
bed. This you may think shows a certain naiveté about man-
woman relationships.

Clive Barnes, *New York Times,* 28 Mar. 1968

Tennessee told me that when he has Lot die, he is killing off all
the wispy, willowy women he has written about, that he wasn't

53

going to write that kind of woman anymore.
Mike Steen, A Look at Tennessee Williams, p. 266

Confessional

Play in one act.
Written: 1967, as first version of *Small Craft Warnings* (see p. 58).
First production: Maine Th. Arts Festival, Bar Harbor, Maine, Summer 1971 (dir. William E. Hunt).
Published: in *Dragon Country;* and in *Theatre, Vol. VII.*

The Two-Character Play

Play in two acts.
Written: as an earlier version of *Out Cry* (see p. 57).
First production: Hampstead Th. Club, London, 12 Dec. 1967 (dir. James Roose-Evans; with Peter Wyndgarde as Felice and Mary Ure as Claire).
First New York production: Quaigh Th., 14 Aug. 1975 (dir. Bill Lentsch; des. Greg Huskinko and Isabelle Harris; with Robert Stattel as Felice and Maryellen Flynn as Claire).
Revived: Call Board Th., Los Angeles, California, 22 Feb. 1977.
Published: New York: New Directions, 1969; and in *Theatre, Vol. V.*

The Two-Character Play *is a private occasion for Williams himself, an obsessive two-hour rant that taxes the actors' memories with tortuous interlocking half-lines and the director's skill in dictating variations of space in a vacuum. . . . A brother and sister arrive in an empty theatre to discover they've been deserted by the touring company to which they belong. . . . They proceed with an incomplete set to mount their own show . . . a torrid Southern drama of aberration and murder with which their own lives are inextricably mingled . . . the only possible finish (though no 'conclusion') lying in the property revolver with which the play-within-the-play's father has killed his wife and then himself. . . .*

What we're evidently confronted with here are several layers of Williams's own life. . . . The play-within-the-play suggests the close relationship between an author and his characters as he feeds them lines, is taken over by them, is torn between their reality and his own reworking of them for an audience. A public performance can only be an inadequate approximation, possibly even a betrayal, of this private world. Furthermore Williams has often spoken of his own claustrophobia and his growing paranoia over adverse audience and critical responses, as well as the murderous demands of the commercial theatre: these fears frame the play's development.

Philip French, New Statesman, 22 Dec. 1967

It would need a psychoanalyst — and preferably Tennessee Williams's own — to offer a rational interpretation of the enigmas that litter the stage like pieces of an elaborate jigsaw.

Herbert Kretzmer, Daily Express, 13 Dec. 1967

If you must say what it is about, say it is a tragedy with laughter. It affirms nothing but gallantry in the face of defeat — but that, I think, is no small thing to affirm in the Pentagon's shadow.

Williams, New York Times, 2 May 1971

Two-Character Play ... he describes as his 'last long play ... conceived and written when I was almost completely phased out, and rewritten several times after my release from the psychiatric hospital, but it is still the work of a very disturbed writer, and it is terribly personal and I don't know how much empathy will be engaged'.

Rex Reed, interviewing Williams, Esquire, Sept. 1971

In the Bar of a Tokyo Hotel

Play in one act.
First New York production: Eastside Playhouse, 11 May 1969
    (dir. Herbert Machiz; des. Neil Peter Jampolis, Stanley
    Simmons, and Hayward Morris; with Anne Meacham as Miriam
    and Donald Madden as Mark).
First London production: 1974-75.
Published: New York: Dramatists Play Service, 1969; in *Dragon
    Country;* and in *Theatre, Vol. VII.*

A portrait of an artist at the nadir of his career. . . . In the turmoil of his nightmare exaltation he experiences the dread sensation of becoming identical with his work. The mess of pigment he applies to his canvases appears to blind him with some unknown but immensely forceful ingredient of light. . . . This may be the prelude to the total disintegration of his talent; or it may possibly mark the threshold of a never-before-attained profundity of insight. The double awareness is killing him. . . . At the end of the play, when the artist dies, his wife, bereft of all attachments and direction, divests herself of the jewelry which represents the acquisitions bestowed upon her by his former success. Only a homosexual art dealer who sponsored the artist's work grieves for him. He agrees that his protege's final paintings ought not to be publicly shown, yet suggests that an artist's passage to a new phase will frequently prove chaotic and undecipherable. He has no intention of exhibiting such paintings, but acknowledges the possibility that a minor gallery (I almost said 'Off-Broadway') might hazard doing so. . . .

Harold Clurman, *The Nation*, 2 June 1969

Mr. Williams has, perhaps, never been overreluctant to show the world his wounds — but in this new play he seems to be doing nothing else. The play repelled me with its self-pity as much as it fascinated me with the author's occasional resurgence of skill. . . . There are bursting, sharp exchanges of dialogue that recall *The Glass Menagerie* in their sudden poignant pertinence. But the philosophic content of the play — which alone could have justified it as something more than clearly successful therapy — is a cotton puffball of commonplace.

Clive Barnes, *New York Times*, 12 May 1969

It is about the usually early and particularly humiliating doom of the artist. He has made, in the beginning of his vocation, an almost total commitment of himself to his work. As Mark truthfully says, the intensity of the work, the unremitting challenges and demands that it makes to him and of him (in most cases daily) leave so little of him after the working hours that simple, comfortable *being* is impossible for him. . . . As death approaches, he hasn't the comfort of feeling with any conviction that any of his work has had any essential value.

Williams, notes to the cast at the Eastside Playhouse

Demolition Downtown

Play in one act.
Written: before 1971.
First production: London, 1977.
Published: in *Esquire,* June 1971.

A short, unreal play about suburbanites at the end of the world.

Out Cry

Play in one act.
Written: as a revised version of *The Two-Character Play* (see
    p. 54).
First production: Ivanhoe Th., Chicago, Illinois, 8 July 1971 (dir.
    George Keathley; with Donald Madden as Felice and Eileen
    Herlie as Clare).
First New York production: Lyceum Th., 1 Mar. 1973 (dir. Peter
    Glenville; des. Jo Mielziner and Sandy Cole; with Michael York
    as Felice and Cara Duff-McCormick as Clare).
Revived: Thirteenth Street Repertory Company, New York City,
    17 June 1974 (dir. Laura Zucker).
Published: New York: New Directions, 1969.

There is a hollow ring to Tennessee Williams's new play, Out
Cry*. . . . It is tragedy on a small scale, so despairing as to be almost
incredible, imbued with a terror that doesn't quite terrorize. . . .
Remnants and reminiscenes of the Tennessee Williams style are
there, and there are more than a few echoes – the shadow of insanity that pervaded* A Streetcar Named Desire, *the recurrent rose
symbol (this time in a worn carpet) from* The Rose Tattoo, *the
brother-sister relationship of* The Glass Menagerie *and the inevitable setting (for no perceptible reason) of the play-within-a-play
in a 'deep Southern town. . .'. A lot of thought and work and
effort went into this Ivanhoe premiere, but one recalls a line of
the brother's in the play when he refers to a 'ponderously*

symbolic undrama'.

William Leonard, *Chicago Tribune,* 9 July 1971

Out Cry is a very brave and very difficult play.... Seen in the context of Broadway show-business, its situation and its poetry, its demands on ears and mind, may seem to many merely pretentious ... yet this is an adventure to drama at which many, perhaps the majority, will scoff ... but some will find stimulating.... Minorities, needless to say, are not always wrong.

Clive Barnes, *New York Times,* 2 Mar. 1973

Despite our anticipating, the play is never as interesting as it sounds. Even after one sees the play, it still *sounds* interesting.

Mel Gussow, *New York Times,* 11 Mar. 1973

Mr. Williams himself, like his Southern heroines, is still, somehow, bravely himself, even in reduced circumstances. And this play is better than some of his later, sadder ones.... *Out Cry* is Mr. Williams's farthest departure from specific time and place since that beautiful dramatic poem, *Camino Real,* and I think the departure has done him some good.

Julius Novick, *Village Voice,* 8 Mar. 1973

[On the change of title to *Out Cry*] It fits so perfectly. I had to *cry out,* and I did. It's the only possible title.... It's the history of what I went through in the 'sixties transmuted into the predicament of a brother and sister.... I think *Out Cry* is my most beautiful play since *Streetcar,* and I've never stopped working on it.

Williams, interviewed by Robert Jennings,
Playboy, April 1973

Small Craft Warnings

Play in two acts.
Written: as an expanded version of *Confessional* (see p. 54).
First New York productions: Truck and Warehouse Th., 2 Apr.
1972; New Th., 6 June 1972 (dir. Richard Altman; des.
Fred Voelpel and John Gleason; with Helena Carroll as Leona,

Gene Fanning as Monk, William Hickey as Steve, and Williams himself – the acting debut of the playwright – as Doc, for the first five performances).

First London production: Hampstead Theatre Club, Jan. 1973 (dir. Vivian Matalon; des. Saul Rodomsky; with Elaine Stritch as Leona, Peter Jones as Monk, and James Berwick as Steve).

Published: New York: New Directions, 1972; London: Secker and Warburg, 1973; and in *Theatre, Vol. V.*

A collection of misfits in a bar change emotional partners and dance through the night.

Crève Coeur

Play in two scenes.
Written: c. 1975.
First production: Spoleto Festival, Charleston, South Carolina, 5 June 1978 (dir. Keith Hack; des. Steve Rubin and Craig Miller; with Shirley Knight as Dorothea and Jan Miner as Bodey).
First New York production: as *A Lovely Sunday for Crève Coeur,* Hudson Guild Th., 10 Jan. 1979 (dir. Keith Hack); with Shirley Knight as Dorothea and Peg Murray as Bodey).
Published: New York: New Directions, 1980.

This is a tale of four women, living in St. Louis in 1935. The central figure is Dorothea ... a transplanted Southerner, no longer young, who teaches civics in a local school. She is the quintessential Williams half-faded rose, still leaning toward the fast-dimming sunlight of romance. It's Sunday, and Dorothea is doing her exercises and waiting for a phone call from her beau, the dashing school principal, who she thinks is going to marry her. You, of course, know better, sniffing those fading roses in the Williams air. ... It's classic Williams chemistry – a tacky and slightly decayed spiritual ambience out of which a sweet, forlorn poetry is to be distilled. ... Instead, you get a quasifarcical humour with gags about premature ejaculation, diarrhoea, and other 'afflictions visited on the gifted', as Dorothea put it at one point. ...

Jack Kroll, *Newsweek*, 5 Feb. 1979

Williams cannot go on indefinitely rehashing his old plays, *Crève Coeur* consisting almost entirely of rechewed bits of *Menagerie* and *Street Car*. ... There is no real drama here. We know from the beginning that Dottie is deluding herself. ... Lazy arbitrariness posing as dramatic necessity is worse . . . than a wolf in sheep's clothing; it is a sheep in wolf's clothing, and fools no-one. ... The kindest thing to assume is that Williams died shortly after completing *Sweet Bird of Youth,* and that his subsequent, ever more dismal plays are the work of a lover of his who has seemed to impersonate him perfectly in daily life, but only very crudely in playwriting. ...

John Simon, *New York,* 26 June 1978

The Red Devil Battery Sign

Play in two acts.
Written: 1975-76.
First productions: Schubert Th., Boston, Massachusetts, 18 June 1976 (dir. Edwin Sherin; des. Robin Wagner, Ruth Wagner and Marilyn Rennagel; with Anthony Quinn as King Del Rey and Claire Bloom as Woman Downtown); English Th., Vienna, Austria, 17 Dec. 1976 (dir. Franz Schafrank; with Keith Baxter as King Del Rey and Ruth Brinkmann as Woman Downtown).
First London production: Roundhouse, 8 June 1977, trans. to Phoenix Th., 7 July 1977 (dir. Keith Baxter and David Leland; des. Bob Ringwood, Kate Owen and David Hersey; with Keith Baxter as King Del Rey and Estelle Kohler as Woman Downtown). *Unpublished.*

Set in Dallas just after the Kennedy assassination, [the] first character we meet is a rich, loud-talking Southern lady known simply as Downtown Woman. She suffers from the usual Williams collection of troubles (sexual itch, alcoholism, incipient insanity). ... One night lurching in the bar of the Yellow Rose Hotel, she's attracted to a swarthy musician now unemployed because he suffers from a brain tumour, and she invites him to her penthouse suite. This gentleman is King Del Rey, late middle-aged, married, and, of course, not of Downtown Woman's class. Let me add here that the metaphoric reversals in these character's names is a suggestion of the pomposity in the writing. . . . King . . . has a talented and sexy daughter whom he has moulded in the direction of stardom. Except she's holed up in Chicago with a lover and is not allowed to come home because her mother thinks there's something unnatural, if not outright incestual, between father and daughter. Anyway, as these cross-relationships cut into each other, with an undue amount of time given to repetitive duologues between King and Downtown Woman, there's a lot of pseudo-poetic talk about 'unhooded eyes and deception', as well as dark intimations about contemporary civilization ('The world doesn't encourage too much sanity lately'). . . .

The real clue to this vacuity may be found in the desperation of the play's plotting . . . the voltage in the symbolism wouldn't light a penlight. . . . When the diversion of the music and the scenery lets up, there are the performances and my-oh-my what a mess!!

Kevin Kelly, *Boston Globe,* 19 June 1976

At Saturday night's preview of Tennessee Williams's new play . . . star Anthony Quinn offered free tickets to audience members who felt cheated. . . . Director Edwin Sherin appeared on stage and told the capacity house that what it was going to see was a 'working rehearsal. . . . Mr. Quinn has asked me to make this explanation to you. If any of you would prefer to come back at some later time during the run, you are welcome to as his guests'. . . . No one took up Quinn's offer. . . .

Boston Globe, 18 June 1976

This Is (An Entertainment)

Play in two acts.
Written: 1976.
First production: Geary Th., San Francisco, California, 20 Jan. 1976 (dir. Allen Fletcher; des. John Jensen, F. Mitchell Dana, and Robert Morgan; with Elizabeth Huddle as the Countess and Ray Reinhardt as the Count). *Unpublished.*

Playing one of Williams's captivating castrators (a nameless Countess in this avatar), [Elizabeth] Huddle cheerfully cuckolds her munitions maker husband. . . . Revolutions may rip a country apart, children and dogs may vanish inexplicably, one lover may be replaced by another, but none of this touches the Countess, who declares ad nauseam 'This is!!' and proceeds to appreciate every passing 'this'. . . . Williams's revolution is simply irrelevant to his single character in a densely populated play.

It is of course possible to laugh at a munitions maker as a crawling sex-starved cuckold, but such figures would look better in *Daily Worker* cartoons than on John Jansen's grateful set. . . . Williams is as irrepressible in his writing as his Countess is in her lechery. I asked him how his plays germinated, and he replied that they grew from the empty page that faced him every morning. . . . Williams is the grand old dramatist of the American theatre, so let us celebrate his plays that are more than entertainment.

Ruby Cohn, *Educational Theatre Journal*, Oct. 1976

Vieux Carré

Play in two acts.
Written: 1970s.
First New York production: St. James Th., 11 May 1977 (dir. Arthur Allen; des. James Tilton and Jane Greenwood; with Richard Alfieri as the Writer, Tom Aldredge as the Painter, and Sylvia Sidney as Mrs. Wire).
First English productions: Playhouse Th., Nottingham, 16 May 1978; Piccadilly Th., London, 9 Aug. 1978 (dir. Keith Hack; des. Voytek; with Karl Johnson as the Writer, Richard Kane as Nightingale, and Sylvia Miles as Mrs. Wire).
Revived: WPA Th., New York, 4 Apr. 1983.
Published: New York: New Directions, 1979.

A gross autobiographical self-indulgence, in which [Williams] takes himself back, Isherwood-like, to his earliest days as a struggling writer in New Orleans [where] he finds the landlady of his life in the form of Mrs. Wire, a dominating figure, as crushing in her motherly affections as in her ruthless approach to her profession. Wire's establishment is inhabited by the complete cast for an undergraduate parody of a Tennessee Williams play. . . . There is Jane, a fallen fashion illustrator from New York, who is shacked up with Tye, an alcoholic gigolo and hustler; there is Mr. Nightingale . . . a homosexual pavement artist and blood-spitting consumptive; there are two distressed gentleladies . . . whose malnutrition gets the better of their genteel airs and dignity. . . .

Tennessee Williams, who appears to have a fondness for ghosts, has often made use of New Orleans in his writings. . . . Mr. Williams has chosen to write the play in the languidly discursive style of his recent experiments in autobiography. . . . The play breathes gently, with an air of politely disguised fatigue . . .

New Yorker, 23 May 1977

Clothes for a Summer Hotel

Play in two acts.
Written: beginning in 1975.
First production: Cort Th., New York, 26 Mar. 1980 (dir.
    Jose Quintero; des. Oliver Smith; with Kenneth Haigh as
    F. Scott Fitzgerald and Geraldine Page as Zelda Fitzgerald).
Published: New York: New Directions, 1983.

All through . . . I kept wondering why Tennessee Williams had written this play about Scott and Zelda Fitzgerald. Surely not to inform us of the details of their lives; there's nothing in the play a reasonably informed adult doesn't know about the double comet of the jazz age, the brilliant novelist and his mercurial, unfulfilled wife who died terribly in a madhouse fire. The action takes place at an asylum in North Carolina, but in reality this 'ghost play', as Williams calls it, seems to be occurring in some spiritual limbo after both Zelda and Scott have died, and so we flash back to the details of these almost legendary lives. The central situation is Zelda's struggle for self-expression, trying to emerge from the shadow of her husband who, she complains, will let her neither write nor dance out of jealousy for her gifts. We see Zelda's infidelity with a French aviator; we see Fitzgerald and Ernest Hemingway exchanging literary and sexual insults; we meet other figures of the legend like Gerald and Sara Murphy and Mrs. Patrick Campbell.

But in dredging up these well-dredged data, Williams adds no deep insights to the lives of these brilliant, self-shattering American figures. Nor is the play moving. . . . The few flashes of Williams's poetry are drowned by language like 'words are the love notes of writers' and there's even a banal echo of Blanche DuBois when Zelda says 'It's the kindness you remember best. The rest is trivia.' Beneath the biographical surface the play may be really about the tension, both creative and lacerating, between the male and female elements in Williams's own psyche. That could have been fruitful and powerful; this play is neither.

Jack Kroll, *Newsweek,* 7 Apr. 1980

The story of a writer embarked on a course of self-destruction after having achieved extraordinary literary success, the story of a man faced with the anguish of caring for a mentally ill relative — these elements in the life of F. Scott Fitzgerald have such close parallels in the life of Tennessee Williams that one hoped his new play might be something in the great Williams tradition. Alas, *Clothes* does nothing to deepen our knowledge of either of the Fitzgeralds, let alone Williams. If the play were not about celebrities, perhaps Williams might have put the material in closer focus. As it is, he has too many opportunities for digressions, like a long, gratuitous scene in which Hemingway repeats overly familiar comments on matters of manhood and literary prowess. . . . [Williams] treats the central character, Zelda, with little sympathy, though her situation has a certain poignancy. . . . Her affecting, ingratiating moments are few. For the most part, she whines. She nags Scott or torments him. It is hard to find her tragic or even sympathetic. . . .

Howard Kissel, *Women's Wear Daily,* 27 Mar. 1980

Tiger Tail

Play in two acts.
Written: 1978, as a stage version of the screenplay *Baby Doll* (see also p. 23 and 27).
First production: Alliance Th., Atlanta, Georgia, Winter 1978 (dir. Harry Rasky; with Elizabeth Kemp as Baby Doll,

Nick Mancuso as Silva, Thomas Toner as Archie Lee, and Mary Nell Santacroce as Aunt Rose). *Unpublished.*

This is the Peaceable Kingdom/ Good Luck God

Play in two scenes.
Unperformed.
Published: Theatre, Vol. VII.

A brother and sister spoon-feed their senile, dying mother while a riot rages in her nursing home.

Steps Must be Gentle

Play in one act.
Unperformed.
Published: in a limited edition, William Targ, 1980.

A dialogue in eerie half-verse between Williams's idol poet, the suicide Hart Crane, and Crane's mother.

Lifeboat Drill

Play in one act.
Unperformed.
Published: Theatre, Vol. VII.

Mr. and Mrs. Taske, a feuding and aged couple, struggle with life preservers in anticipation of the inevitable.

Will Mr. Merriweather Return from Memphis?

Play in two acts.
First production: Tennessee Williams Performing Arts Center, Florida Keys Community College, 25 January 1980.
Unpublished.

It tells of two widows in Bethesda, Miss., who bring alive the past by conjuring up apparitions of such characters as Vincent van Gogh and Arthur Rimbaud. . . . The play draws its name from a former boarder who moved away and left unsatisfied the lust of one of the widows.

New York Times, 26 Jan. 1980

A House Not Meant to Stand

Play in two acts.
Written: beginning *c.*1980.
First production: in a one-act 'workshop version', as *Some Problems for the Moose Lodge,* Goodman's Studio Th., Chicago, Nov. 1980; under its final title, Goodman Th., Chicago, Apr. 1981, and 8 May 1982 (dir. Andre Ernotte; des. Karen Schultz; with Peg Murray as Bella and Frank Hamilton as Cornelius).
Revived: New World Festival of the Arts, Miami, Florida, June 1982. *Unpublished.*

It is a loud, harsh, bitter, pain-filled shriek at the degenerative process of life. . . . The play is ripe with words and images that describe creeping corruption, waste, illness, lunacy, deterioration, and senility. The members of the haunted McCorkle family, as battered as the wreck of the house in which they live, are vicious, aberrant, worn out, or sick unto death . . . bloated with desire for beauty, money, sex, or youth, and in their hunger they gorge themselves on food and drink and pills, becoming physically and mentally gross. In revulsion for this decadent present and in sorrow for the ruined past, the play presents a brief, closing vision that contrasts the shining beginning of innocence with a bleak, wicked end of gluttony and callousness. . . .

The central character, the pathetic mother Bella, is sadly under-developed, and her husband, the ranting Cornelius, is abruptly dropped. There are great lengths of ranting repetition alternating with disconnected, unprepared, unfulfilled moments. And the stinging fury of Williams's poetry, which hits with brutal force in some of the enraged monologues, is mixed with cheap laughs. . . .

In a few scenes ... the play begins to develop the Gothic comic momentum its author intended ... [but] the ending, despite that dazzling final image, is overplotted and underwritten....

Richard Christiansen, *Chicago Tribune,* 28 Apr. 1982

I think the 'German expressionist' treatment was right for my material. I hadn't realized how far I had departed from realism in my writing. I had long since exhausted the so-called 'poetic realism.' This, after all, isn't twenty years ago. I always write to satisfy myself; so I'm not conscious, perhaps, of the change in my work.

Williams, interviewed by Richard Christiansen, *Chicago Tribune,*
9 May 1982

Dakin [Williams] later told his collaborator [Shepherd Mead] that Cornelius was definitely based on himself. 'Were you angry?' 'No, no!' he said, laughing. 'He's used everybody else in the family. It was time he used me.'

Williams and Mead, *Tennessee Williams,* p. 332

Now, the Cats with Jeweled Claws

Play in one act.
Written: 1981.
Unperformed.
Published: in *Theatre, Vol. VII.*

A surreal little play, a quiet bacchanal, in which the dancers are two bitchy matrons and a pair of doomed male hustlers.

Something Cloudy, Something Clear

Play in two acts.
First production: Jean Cocteau Repertory at the Bouwerie Th.,
24 Aug. 1981 (dir. Eve Adamson; des. Douglas McKeown;
with Craig Smith as August and Elton Cormier as Kip).
Unpublished.

Set in Provincetown in 1940, it is based closely on the playwright's own experiences during that 'pivotal summer when I took sort of a crash course in growing up. . .'. It was there that he met his 'first great male' love – a young Canadian draft dodger named Kip. The two lived together briefly in a two-storey shack on Captain Jack's Wharf until one day a girl entered the picture, and Kip told the playwright that their own affair was over. Mr. Williams left immediately for Mexico; he learned later that Kip was dying of a brain tumour. . . . Although a woman who is the mistress of a New York gangster has been added, and Mr. Williams's name has been changed to August, the plot remains surprisingly faithful to the actual story . . .

Michiko Kakutani, *New York Times,* 13 Aug. 1981

Perhaps the play is something in the way of an elegy memorial for and an apology to Kip, in which Williams pictures himself for once not as the poet pining for a doomed love, but the unscrupulous, horny bastard on the make; in effect, the playwright as stinker. . . . Only the minor characters are signs that Williams is still capable of more than alternately wallowing in sentiment and kicking himself for the falseness of his wallow. . . .

Michael Feingold, *Village Voice,* 16 Sept. 1981

a: Fiction

Novels

The Roman Spring of Mrs. Stone. New York: New
    Directions, 1950, 1969; New American Library, 1952,
    1961; Bantam Books, 1976; Toronto: McClelland and
    Stewart, 1969; London: John Lehmann, 1950; Secker
    and Warburg, 1957; Panther Books, 1977.
Moise and the World of Reason. New York: Simon and
    Schuster, 1975; Bantam Books, 1976; London: W.H.
    Allen, 1976. [A sad autobiographical novel, in which
    Williams appears in three guises and at least two
    genders, and appraises love, fame, art and himself.
    The book was billed as a startling and frank discussion
    of homosexuality, and it is, but it is more a revelation
    of the playwright than of the practice.]
The Bag People. New York: Dodd, 1982.

Short Stories

One Arm and Other Stories. New York: New Directions,
    1948; revised version 1954; Toronto: McClelland and
    Stewart, 1967. [Contains stories relating to *The Glass
    Menagerie* ('Portrait of a Girl in Glass'), *Vieux Carré*
    ('The Angel in the Alcove'), and, in the 1954 edition,
    Summer and Smoke ('The Yellow Bird').]
Hard Candy: a Book of Stories. New York: New
    Directions, 1954, 1959, 1967; Toronto: McClelland
    and Stewart, 1967. [Includes 'Three Players of a
    Summer Game' (see *Cat on a Hot Tin Roof*).]
Three Players of a Summer Game, and Other Stories.
    London: Secker and Warburg, 1960; Harmondsworth:
    Penguin Books, 1965. [Contains many of the same
    stories as *Hard Candy,* above.]
The Knightly Quest: a Novella and Four Short Stories.
    New York: New Directions, 1966; London: Secker
    and Warburg, 1968 (with *Twelve Short Stories*).
    [Both versions contain 'Man Bring This Up Road'
    (the story on which *The Milk Train Doesn't Stop
    Here Anymore* elaborates) and 'Kingdom of Earth'
    (as in *Kingdom of Earth*).]
Eight Mortal Ladies Possessed: a Book of Stories. New
    York: New Directions, 1974; Toronto: McClelland and
    Stewart, 1974; London: Secker and Warburg, 1974.

It Happened the Day the Sun Rose, and Other Stories. New
   York: Simon and Schuster, 1982.

b: Poems

In the Winter of Cities: Poems, edited with the help of William S.
   Gray. Norfolk, Connecticut: New Directions, 1956; revised,
   with additional poems, Norfolk, Connecticut: New Directions,
   1964.
Androgyne, Mon Amour: Poems. New York: New Directions,
   1977; Toronto: McClelland and Stewart, 1967.

A sombre play has to be very spare and angular. When you fill it out it seems blotchy, pestilential. You must keep the lines sharp and clean — tragedy is austere. You get the effect, with fewer lines than you are inclined to use.

Notes, 'The Macon Period', Macon, Georgia, Summer 1942, included in *Remember Me to Tom,* p.134.

I have come to the roughest part of a new play, assembling the scattered papers and getting ready to prepare a last draft of it. . . . The ultimate arrangement is a colossal job, which I do with actual groans and muttered curses, sitting on the floor with papers all about me, gradually going into little separate stacks, some order finally emerging, but not till I have died a thousand deaths. I am sure it is worse than child-birth. Reading through it after the assembly is worse still. In fact I usually don't do it, that is why such odd incongruities and contradictions occur in my scripts. Writing is not a happy profession.

Letter to Donald Windham, MGM Pictures, Culver City, California, July 1943, included in *Letters to Donald Windham*

My nerves are tied in knots today. I have plunged into one of my periodic neuroses ... they are a Williams family trait, I suppose. Destroyed my sister's mind and made my father a raging drunkard. In me they take the form of little interior storms that show remarkably little from the outside but which create a deep chasm between myself and all other people, even deeper than the relatively ordinary ones of homosexuality and being an artist.

Letter to Donald Windham, Metro-Goldwyn-Mayer, Culver City, California, 28 July 1943, included in *Letters to Donald Windham*

These professors who write verse and criticism of verse and everything else do not realize that there are a number of artists who cannot teach school and yet have to eat, drink, wear clothes, and live in houses or at least rooms of houses, and who need a bit of comfort and dignity in their lives in order to bear them. From the haven of the academy the rough edges of the problem are not apparent. I know them all too well, I have all but killed myself contending with them for a good many years. The only answer is toughness and more toughness. That is how alligators were made through many years, not one healthy poet in the duration of his lifetime.

> Letter to Donald Windham, Clayton, Missouri, April 1946,
> included in *Letters to Donald Windham*

The audience was sitting absolutely seriously and watching this thing [*Portrait of a Madonna*] which was rather dramatic. And Irene [Selznick] said there was one person in the audience who was screaming with laughter. And much to her surprise it was Tennessee. Screaming with laughter. And she looked at him and he said 'But don't you think it's funny? It's so funny. It's so terribly funny.'

> George Cukor to Mike Steen, *A Look at Tennessee Williams*

For a writer who is not intentionally obscure, and never, in his opinion, obscure at all, I do get asked a hell of a lot of questions which I can't answer. I have never been able to say what was the theme of my play and I don't think I've ever been conscious of writing with a theme in mind. I am always surprised when, after a play has opened, I read in the papers what the play is about. . . . I am thankful for these highly condensed and stimulating analyses, but it would never have occurred to me that that was the story I was trying to tell. Usually when asked about a theme, I look vague and say, 'It is a play about life. . .'.

> 'Questions Without Answers', *New York Times*, 3 Oct. 1948,
> reprinted in *Where I Live*

Tennessee Williams once modestly described himself as a 'minor artist' who has happened to write one or two major works. 'I can't even say', he added, 'which they are'.

> Dan Sullivan, *New York Times*, 21 Oct. 1966

All my life I have been haunted by the obsession that to desire a thing or to love a thing intensely is to place yourself in a vulnerable position, to be a possible, if not a probable, loser of what you most want. . . . My chance of getting, or achieving, anything that I long for will always be gravely reduced by the interminable existence of that block . . . having, always, to contend with this adversary of fear, which was sometimes terror, gave me a certain tendency toward an atmosphere of hysteria and violence in my writing, an atmosphere that has existed in it since the beginning.

'Williams's Wells of Violence', *New York Times,* 8 Mar. 1959,
reprinted in *Where I Live*

The POV [point of view] I am speaking for is just this: that no significant area of human experience, and behaviour reaction to it, should be held inaccessible, provided it is presented with honest intention and taste. . . . The rallying cry of those who want our creative heads on the chopping block is: let's have plays affirming the essential dignity of mankind. It's a damned good platform. The only trouble with it . . . is that we are not agreed about exactly what that high-sounding slogan means. . . . It is not the essential dignity but the essential ambiguity of man that I think needs to be stated.

'Tennessee Williams Presents his POV', *New York Times,*
12 June 1960, reprinted in *Where I Live*

You know I am going to be reviewed more than the play, and that is how it has been for the last ten years.

Letter to Bill Barnes, his agent, on the opening of
Small Craft Warnings, New Orleans, 13 Dec. 1971

Is it or is it not right or wrong for a playwright to put his persona into his work? − My answer is 'What else can he do?' − I mean the very root-necessity of all creative work is to express those things most involved in his experience. Otherwise, is the work, however well executed, not a manufactured, synthetic thing? I've said, perhaps repeatedly, that I have two major classifications for writing: that which is organic and that which is not.

'Too Personal?', preface to *Small Craft Warnings*

Maybe they weren't punks at all, but New York drama critics. Commenting on his experiences at the hands of anti-gay locals of Key West, Florida (his gardener was murdered, his house ransacked, and his dog stolen. Williams himself was mugged twice). To Madeleine H. Blais of the *Chicago Tribune*, 9 Apr. 1979

In my early plays, there was a great rush of emotion backed up in me that found release. In the later plays, I had to dig deeper, and people were always comparing those plays, which were quite different, with the early work. . . . Under these conditions, the new plays suffered.
To Richard Christiansen of the *Chicago Tribune*, 5 Apr. 1981

I think the 'German expressionist' treatment was right for my material. I hadn't realized how far I had departed from realism in my writing. I had long since exhausted the so-called 'poetic realism'. This, after all, isn't twenty years ago. I always write to satisfy myself; so I'm not conscious, perhaps, of the change in my work.
On the opening of *Some Problems for the Moose Lodge*, to Richard Christiansen of the *Chicago Tribune*, 9 May 1982

I've nothing to conceal. Homosexuality isn't the theme of my plays. They're about all human relationships. I've never faked it.
Interview with Arthur Bell, *Village Voice*, 24 Feb. 1972

Why did the critics turn on me so violently in the 'fifties and the early 'sixties? I suspect it was a cabal to cut me down to what they thought was my size. And what is my size? It is, I trust, the size of an artist who has consistently given all that he has to give to his work, with a most peculiar passion. . . . Jesus, career, it's never been that to me, it has just been 'doing my thing' with a fury to do it the best that I am able.
Memoirs, p. 173

[Discussing *Small Craft Warnings*] It wasn't Doc, the part I played, but Quentin, the homosexual, with whom I identified. . . . Like

Quentin, I had [in 1967, when the play was first written as *Confessional*] quite lost the capacity for astonishment.... I'm not a typical homosexual. I can identify completely with Blanche — we are both hysterics — with Alma and even with Stanley.... If you understand schizophrenia, I am not really a *dual* creature; but I can understand the tenderness of women and the lust and libido of the male, which are, unfortunately, too seldom combined in women. That's why I seek out the androgynous, so I can get both.

[*Can't you forget about the critics?*] I've forgotten about them, baby. I wish they'd forget about me.... the critics still want me to be a poetic realist, and I never was. All my *great* characters are larger than life, not realistic. In order to capture the quality of life in two and a half hours everything has to be concentrated, intensified. You must catch life in moments of crisis, moments of electric confrontation. In reality, life is very *slow*.

To Robert Jennings, *Playboy*, Apr. 1973

I think some works of mine, like *Sweet Bird,* are now seen more for other values than the sensational. People today are more accustomed to scenes of sex and violence; they can see a play like *Sweet Bird of Youth* more objectively....

You can say which plays *you* like best, but that doesn't mean they *are* the best. The last person to talk about his work is the author, you know? ... My reaction to the plays shifts continuously....

Anyone who knows me at all knows that I have no need to disguise the sexual nature of my characters. Why would I? ... Sexuality is a part of my work, of course, because sexuality is a part of my life and everyone's life. I see no essential difference between the love of two men for each other and the love of a man for a woman; no essential difference, and that's why I've examined them both....

I have no animosity toward women. I tend to regard them as inviolable — like sisters and mothers....

A lot of our younger playwrights are castrated by the system in which they work. The public isn't conditioned to have the patience to allow them to develop as artists.

To Robert Berkvist, *New York Times,* 21 Dec. 1975

I assure you that the South is the country of my heart as well as my birth. If I were writing about Yankees, I promise you I would find every bit as much 'damnation' among them — and not as much charm! ... I don't think of my little people as damned not as long as they keep courage and gallantry. Those are important and very Southern qualities, bred in the bones of the people I write about. ...

I write out of love for the South. But I can't expect Southerners to realize that my writing about them is an expression of love. It is out of a regret for a South that no longer exists that I write of the forces that have destroyed it. ... There is still the Cavalier tradition the North never had and less of the dog-eat-dog attitude, though it disturbs me to find the South so conservative in its social point of view.

Quoted in *Remember Me to Tom,* p. 213

I'm very conscious of my decline in popularity ... but I don't permit it to stop me because I have the example of so many playwrights before me. I know the dreadful notices Ibsen got. ... To me it has been providential to be an artist, a great act of Providence that I was able to turn my borderline psychosis into creativity — my sister Rose did not manage this. So I keep writing. ...

To Michiko Kakatani, *New York Times,* 13 Aug. 1981

I presume to insist there must be somewhere truth to be pursued each day with words that are misunderstood and feared because they are the words of an Artist, which must always remain a word most compatible with the word Revolutionary, and so be more than a word.

'The Misunderstanding and Fears of an Artist's Revolt', in *Where I Live*

a: Primary Sources
Collection of Plays

Twenty-Seven Wagons Full of Cotton, and other One-Act Plays. Norfolk, Connecticut: New Directions, 1945; London: Grey Walls Press, 1947; John Lehmann, 1949. [*This Property is Condemned; The Purification; The Last of My Solid Gold Watches; Auto-da-Fé; The Strangest Kind of Romance; Twenty-Seven Wagons Full of Cotton; The Lady of Larkspur Lotion; Hello from Bertha; Portrait of a Madonna; Lord Byron's Love Letter; The Long Goodbye.* A revised edition published by New Directions in 1953, and in 1966 by New Directions and McClelland and Stewart, includes Williams's essay on the St. Louis Mummers ('Something Wild') and the one-act plays *Talk To Me Like the Rain and Let Me Listen* and *Something Unspoken.*]

American Blues: Five Short Plays. New York; London: Dramatists Play Service, 1948. [*Moony's Kid Don't Cry; Ten Blocks of the Camino Real; The Case of the Crushed Petunias; The Dark Room; The Long Stay Cut Short.*]

Four Plays. London: Secker and Warburg, 1956. [*The Glass Menagerie, A Streetcar Named Desire, Summer and Smoke, Camino Real.*]

Five Plays. London: Secker and Warburg, 1962. [*Cat on a Hot Tin Roof; The Rose Tattoo; Something Unspoken; Suddenly Last Summer; Orpheus Descending.*]

Dragon Country: a Book of Plays. New York: New Directions, 1969; Toronto: McClelland and Stewart, 1969. [*In the Bar of a Tokyo Hotel; I Rise in Flame, Cried the Phoenix; The Mutilated; I Can't Imagine Tomorrow; Confessional; The Frosted Glass Coffin; The Gnädiges Fräulein; A Perfect Analysis Given by a Parrot.*]

The Theatre of Tennessee Williams. New York: New Directions; Toronto: McClelland and Stewart.
Volume I, 1971: *Battle of Angels; The Glass Menagerie; A Streetcar Named Desire.*
Volume II, 1971: *The Eccentricities of a Nightingale; Summer and Smoke; The Rose Tattoo;*

           Camino Real.

Volume III, 1971: *Cat on a Hot Tin Roof; Orpheus Descending; Suddenly Last Summer.*

Volume IV, 1972: *Sweet Bird of Youth; Period of Adjustment; The Night of the Iguana.*

Volume V, 1976: *The Milk Train Doesn't Stop Here Anymore; Kingdom of Earth/The Seven Descents of Myrtle; Small Craft Warnings; The Two-Character Play.*

Volume VI, 1976: *Twenty-Seven Wagons Full of Cotton and Other Plays* (contents as for individual volume, above).

Volume VII, 1976: *In The Bar of a Tokyo Hotel; I Rise in Flame, Cried the Phoenix; The Mutilated; I Can't Imagine Tomorrow; Confessional; The Frosted Glass Coffin; The Gnädiges Fräulein; A Perfect Analysis Given by a Parrot; Lifeboat Drill; Now, the Cats with Jeweled Claws; This is the Peaceable Kingdom, or Good Luck God.*

Essays, Letters, and Interviews

Tennessee Williams' Letters to Donald Windham 1940-1965, edited with comments by Donald Windham. New York: Holt, Rinehart, and Winston, 1976. [An invaluable collection of letters which illuminates Williams's pre-success. Contains particularly interesting details on *The Glass Menagerie* en route to Broadway.]

Rex Reed, 'Tennessee Williams Turns Sixty', *Esquire,* 76 (Sept. 1971), p. 105-08, 216-23. [Interview.]

C. Robert Jennings, '*Playboy* Interview: Tennessee Williams', *Playboy,* XX (Apr. 1973), p. 69-84.

Memoirs. Garden City, N.Y.: Doubleday, 1975; London: W.H. Allen, 1976. [Williams later complained that his autobiography was trimmed by the publishers to place undue emphasis on his sex life, and this aspect of the book did receive most of the considerable attention. However, as in the case of *Moise* (see above, p. 69), to dismiss the book as publicity-garnering fluff would be unfair. The student seeking the playwright's illuminating thoughts on specific works will be disappointed, but the playwright on the *playwright* is well worth the time it takes to plough through the erotic miscellany. It is particularly worthwhile to read *Memoirs* in conjunction with *Letters to Donald Windham,* and to note the effects of thirty years.]

Victoria Radin, 'Fighting off the Furies', *The Observer,* London,

22 May 1977, p. 22. [Interview.]

Where I Live: Selected Essays, edited by Christine R. Day and
Bob Woods, with an introduction by Christine R. Day. New
York: New Directions, 1978; Toronto: McClelland and
Stewart, 1978. [Essays on subjects as diverse as Carson
McCullers and Tallulah Bankhead; Williams on his major plays,
reprinted as they appeared in the *New York Times;* and
musings on the nature and vagaries of success.]

b: Secondary Sources

Full-length Studies

Donald Windham, *The Hero Continues.* New York: Thomas Y.
Crowell, 1960. [A *roman a clef,* in which Denis Freeman
corresponds, more or less, to Tennessee Williams. An
interesting book to read after the nonfictional works.]

Edwina Dakin Williams, with Lucy Freeman, *Remember Me to
Tom.* New York: G.P. Putnam's Sons, 1963; London: Carroll,
1964. [Tennessee's brother Dakin Williams maintains in *his*
biography (see below) that the playwright had great
objections to *Remember Me to Tom.* This book, by their
mother Edwina, the original Amanda of *Menagerie,* portrays
her husband Cornelius in a bad light. However one feels about
Cornelius, Edwina's digressions on her Old Southern girlhood
are fascinating, and the book also contains extracts from
Tennessee's early work journals, correspondence, and much
loving and totally subjective commentary on the son and his
plays. The reader who grows weary of the playwright's busy
sex life may read *Remember* with a sense of relief; the ladylike
Miss Edwina mentions her son's long-time lover, Frank Merlo,
exactly once.]

Gilbert Maxwell, *Tennessee Williams and Friends: an Informal
Biography.* Cleveland, Ohio: World Publishing Co., 1965. [As
a study of Williams, this chatty tome is an excellent biography
of Gilbert Maxwell.]

Mike Steen, *A Look at Tennessee Williams.* New York:
Hawthorn, 1969. [This first 'biography' of Williams is a
collection of interviews done by Steen. The interviewees range
from actors and actresses, creators of roles in Williams's plays, to
friends of the playwright. Like Maxwell's, Steen's book tells as
much about the author and interviewees as about the
ostensible subject, but Steen's is less directly personal and

more lively.]

Richard F. Leavitt, *The World of Tennessee Williams*. New York: G.P. Putnam's Sons, 1978; London: W.H. Allen, 1978. [This otherwise pedestrian biography is noteworthy for two reasons: the foreword, written by Williams (apparently rather grudgingly) and the numerous programmes, playbills, and reviews that serve to 'illustrate' the book.]

Dakin Williams and Shepherd Mead, *Tennessee Williams: an Intimate Biography*. New York: Arbor House, 1983. [Notable chiefly as an update to Williams's own *Memoirs*.]

Critical Essays

Among the huge quantity of secondary literature on Tennessee Williams, Robert Bechtold Heilman's *The Iceman, the Arsonist, and the Troubled Agent* (Seattle, Washington: University of Washington Press, 1973), and Gore Vidal's 'Selected Memories of the Glorious Bird and the Golden Age' (*New York Review of Books*, 5 Feb. 1976, p. 13-18) may be especially recommended. The three collections below assemble a representative assortment of academic criticism.

Jordan Miller, ed., *Twentieth Century Interpretations of A Streetcar Named Desire: a Collection of Critical Essays*. Englewood Cliffs, N.J.: Prentice-Hall, 1971. [Contemporary reviews, and 20 other essays including a selection from Elia Kazan's director's notes.]

Stephen Stanton, ed., *Tennessee Williams: a Collection of Critical Essays*. Englewood Cliffs, N.J.: Prentice-Hall, 1977. [Sixteen essays drawn from the period 1964 to 1977.]

Jac Tharpe, ed., *Tennessee Williams: a Tribute*. Jackson: University of Mississippi Press, 1977. [A huge, 896-page collection, assembling 53 essays on Williams.]

Reference Sources

Drewey Wayne Gunn, *Tennessee Williams: a Bibliography*. Metuchen, N.J.: Scarecrow Press, 1980. [Full details of primary sources, interviews, essays, and academic studies.]

John S. McCann, *The Critical Reputation of Tennessee Williams: a Reference Guide*. Boston: G.K. Hall, 1983. [Fully annotated listing of all forms of secondary literature.]